PRAISE FOR *THRIVING THROUGH TOUGH TIMES*

Living is not for the faint of heart, and life is tough even in the best of times. So how do we learn to strengthen our hearts and cultivate the courage not only to survive but even to thrive? This is the question Deidre Combs answers in *Thriving through Tough Times*. Her prescriptions are clear, compelling, and cogent. After reading this book, you have no excuse for not living fully, or, if you do, read it again.

—Rabbi Rami Shapiro,
author of the *Sacred Art of Lovingkindness*

I read Deidre's book when I was walking through the hardest two years of my life. So many things were falling apart, and I felt lost, frightened, and alone. I was in pain, and the worst of it was that I didn't know what to do, where to begin, or how to make it better.

Reading Deidre's book was like being sent a lifeline. Her map of the four seasons of loss gave me understanding, hope, and solace. The metaphor gave me a new perspective on my pain, which eased much of my anxiety and panic. I felt less alone. I didn't take my hard time so personally. I realized, We all go through these seasons. It's not my fault.

Deidre's wise words gave me structure—a plan—when I was caught in a tailspin and felt lost about what to do. She took me by the hand, and I was able to take the next step, and then the next, and then the next.... Her book was an invaluable guide in helping me find my way back home, and I highly recommend it for anyone who finds themselves in a hurting, tender place.

—Karly Randolph Pitman, author of *Overcoming Sugar Addiction*

Wow—this is a great book! Buy it. Read it. Use it. You'll thank me.

—David Baum, PhD, DMin, author of *Lightning in a Bottle and The Randori Principles*

To date there is no other more practical and inspirational guide that can provide the comfort, understanding, hope and wisdom that this book does for facing and moving through challenging ordeals. This book is filled with common perennial wisdom for all to use and apply in any circumstance.

—Angeles Arrien, Ph.D. Cultural Anthropologist, author of *The Second Half of Life and Living in Gratitude*

Times of change and transition can be extremely difficult. Deidre Combs offers practical and heartfelt guidance to help readers stay open and grounded as they go through this often-turbulent time in their lives. *Thriving through Tough Times* offers a wealth of information interlaced with meaningful quotes, stories and useful tools.

Using four seasons and linking them to eight practical strategies she invites readers to meet the complexities of their unique journey with trust, courage and compassion. This creates a rich broth of wisdom and knowledge that will bring both comfort and nourishment to those dealing with change and uncertainty.

This book is both well written and inspiring. I highly recommend it.

—Victoria Crawford, author of *The Art & Practice of Trust: Finding Your Way through Uncertainty, Change and Transition*

THRIVING THROUGH TOUGH TIMES

THRIVING THROUGH TOUGH TIMES

Eight Cross-Cultural Strategies to Navigate Life's Ordeals

DEIDRE COMBS

Author photo by Thomas Lee

Illustrations by Paul Gorsuch

Except for certain friends and family, names, characteristics and story details have been changed to protect the identities of those who inspired this book.

ISBN: 1466202998
ISBN 13: 9781466202993

Library of Congress Control Number: 2011914082
CreateSpace, North Charleston, SC

For Bruce.

To exist is to change, to change is to mature,
to mature is to go on creating oneself endlessly.

— HENRI BERGSON

CONTENTS

Introduction i

Chapter 1: To Everything There Is a Season 1
Summary of the Four Stages 8

Autumn

Chapter 2: Get a Team 17
Chapter 3: Believe in a Happy Ending 37

Winter

Chapter 4: Give Yourself a Break 59
Chapter 5: Eat, Drink, Play, Laugh 81

Spring

Chapter 6: Celebrate 103
Chapter 7: Mark the End and a New Beginning 115

Summer

Chapter 8: Give Back to Come Back 133

Conclusion 147

Tough-Times Classics 155
Queen Inanna's Descent into the Underworld 157

Notes 161
Acknowledgments 185
About the Author 187

INTRODUCTION

Difficulty, my brethren, is the nurse of greatness—
a harsh nurse, who roughly rocks her foster-children
into strength and athletic proportion.

—WILLIAM CULLEN BRYANT (1794–1878)

Once upon a time, you were born. As you grew up, you probably set out into the world and found a job and a place to live. You may have gained a partner and raised some children. Heck, you may have acquired some money, made a passel of friends, and became well respected. You created a routine where you went to work, bought groceries, and paid taxes. Until one day, something changes.

If we stick around long enough, significant change comes our way. Children grow up. Financial markets go up and go down. Relationships end and people die. Organizations falter or they become enormously successful. Our bodies age. International borders shift, and governments turn over. We sometimes get really sick. Things change, and, often, change is not welcome.

Living is like swimming in the ocean. Being born, you dip your toes in the water. If you are brave enough to fall in love or go to work, you dive in and ride the incoming breakers. Amuse yourself in those easy waves long enough, and you will encounter surprise swells that knock you off your feet and spin you under.

When unwelcome changes hit your personal beach, usually you can knock the liquid from your ears and stumble back to standing, such as when you lose a job but are able to find new employment. We don't enjoy these experiences, but we recover. We chalk up the pitfall as a good learning exercise, and are willing to dive back in.

I define the tough times that this book covers as those really rough spots when you don't want to play in life's water anymore. It is when you have been careful and have tried to do everything right, but roaring life waves nail you, fill your sinuses, and twist you so terribly that you lose your orientation. These are the times when, finally able to grasp a breath and tread water, you realize that you have been set adrift.

Tough times appear when the people, health, or bank accounts we counted on disappear. We suddenly lose someone very dear. We become really, really ill, or the bank auctions our home. We could also name these periods "when things fall apart" or "when the ground dissolves underneath our feet." After a friend's house burned to the ground, turning all her belongings to ash, she described these circumstances as when no amount of positive thinking or prayer makes it better. Basically, life gets lousy, and there is nothing you can do to change it.

> *Adversity causes some men to break; others to break records.*
>
> — WILLIAM A. WARD

After a turbulent divorce, long financial hardship, and other unwelcome surprises, losing her home became almost comical to my friend. She said, "If the gods have sent me all this to teach me something, I hope I figure it out quick, because this is getting ridiculous." During tough times, we, like this wise friend, can feel like the biblical character Job or the heroes of ancient Greek tragedies who scream at the sky saying, "Why me?" and "You are destroying this too? You've got to be kidding."

Since 1994, I have researched, written about, and taught cross-cultural approaches to resolving conflict. I mediate and facilitate when groups are battling. I'm passionate about finding the opportunities hidden within any dispute. It's no surprise that one day, in the midst of a set of my own tough times, I remembered that situations like these have historically been described as a disagreement with the gods. I thought, "Maybe I can use my global dispute resolution skills to battle with what life is dishing out." Not only did I find my conflict skills extremely helpful for coping with my personal troubles, they also have proved effective for helping my clients overcome their most difficult challenges.

> *Suffering is the sandpaper of our life. It does its work of shaping us. Suffering is part of our training program for becoming wise.*
>
> — RAM DASS

To verify what might be the top cross-cultural strategies for surviving tough times, I tapped another common tough-times metaphor. When the world you live in essentially ends (people leave, businesses fail, health disappears, etc.), and you are lucky enough to land in a new existence, societies around the world compare this to a *death and rebirth.* I thus searched for common themes and strategies in our global death and mourning rituals. What I found turned out to be a great resource, because humans have practiced coping with loss of life for thousands of years. By integrating sixteen years of cross-cultural conflict research with the world's ubiquitous death—and possible rebirth—practices, I arrived at eight practical and tested techniques.

When we are in the middle of tough times, necessary support often appears. As Jenni Lowe-Anker wrote in her book *Forget Me Not*, after her alpinist husband Alex Lowe was killed in an avalanche in Tibet, "I awoke each day to the shock of its reality; I wanted nothing more than to claw my way back into sleep and my dreams, where there wasn't a pit of fear in my stomach and a heavy weight on my chest…I wanted only to stay in my bed and cry." In her early forties, Jenni lost her husband, mother, and sister within a two-year period. She had been broken apart, and we in her community knew she needed help. It was time to check in, bring food, and support a gentle recovery. We all knew, Jenni included, that she was in tough times, and we helped to ease her journey through them.

However, we can get set adrift by more subtle changes. Financial insecurity, a disrupted workplace, or a troubled marriage can throw us into turmoil. Dealing with a child with special needs can throw us over the edge, or it can be seemingly harmless news that sends us into terribly dark waters. Deena had grown up believing that her parents had loved each other and enjoyed raising her. During their bitter divorce, her father said that much of her childhood had been a chore. She was devastated. If her parents' marriage and their commitment to her had been a farce, how else had she deluded herself? Because she was married with children of her own, she thought that her parent's' divorce shouldn't be a big deal, but she said, "I feel my entire life up until now has been a lie."

When we lose solid ground for whatever reason, we can begin to question everything. Deena added questions like, "What, if anything, can I really trust?" and "If this could happen, what else is possible?"

> *Let me not pray to be sheltered from dangers, but to be fearless in facing them. Let me not beg for the stilling of my pain, but for the heart to conquer it.*
>
> —RABINDRANATH TAGORE

Our reality feels like a falling house of cards, even though external reality appears relatively unchanged. Like Deena, we may have to continue through the paces of everyday life, but it feels like a tsunami has had its way with our insides.

Helen Keller described this experience:

> It was a terrible blow to my faith when I learned that millions of my fellow creatures must labor all their days for food and shelter, bear the most crushing burdens, and die without having known the joy of living. My security vanished forever, and I have never regained [the] belief of my young years that earth is a happy home and hearth for the majority of mankind...When I think of the suffering and famine, and the continued slaughter of men, my spirit bleeds.

Without a major tragedy like Jenni's, our inner turmoil can be embarrassing. We are often ashamed that others bounce back from war, famine, and tsunamis while we are vanquished by relatively small bumps in a pretty comfortable road. How could Deena complain about making bad assumptions about her upbringing when others were burying their children or starving to death? To add to the internal personal crisis, we can feel like complete idiots. We wonder how we might have missed the obvious and been so naïve. We had told ourselves that we were safe because we were smart, young, and healthy, or good parents or dutiful spouses. Caught off guard by tough times, we can lose a core sense of identity or safety and be left feeling thoroughly downtrodden for months or years.

Denying or hiding our difficulties just makes them worse. As you will read in the following chapters, to get our lives back on track, we need to both face and 'fess up about our struggles. We are in good company: swim long enough, and a pounding wave is sure to come everyone's way. As the Buddhist teacher Pema Chödrön wisely states, "It doesn't really matter what causes us to reach our limit. The point is that sooner or later it happens to all of us." Over thousands of years, our forbearers were knocked down and pulled under and had to figure out ways to find solid ground.

To offer support to children and grandchildren, generations of survivors have shared eight strategies—hiding them in cultural practices, stories, and kitchen-table wisdom—which have become commonly accepted recovery techniques across the world. One of these will serve as an overlying structure for this book.

CHAPTER 1

To Everything There Is a Season

To everything there is a season, a time for every purpose under the sun. A time to be born and a time to die; a time to plant and a time to pluck up that which is planted; a time to kill and a time to heal.

—ECCLESIASTES 3:1-3

After I finished presenting a keynote lecture on surviving difficult circumstances, a soft-spoken grandmother approached me and said, "When you described tough times as having four different seasons, you had my attention."

My new acquaintance had raised children and crops in New Mexico and northern Canada. She said, "When the kids were young and we were really struggling as farmers and parents, I copied and pasted a passage from Ecclesiastes on my cupboard." She began to recite, "To everything there is a season, a time for every purpose under the sun…"

This tough rancher explained, "There were times when it made sense to roll up your sleeves and try to fix a problem, but there were also times when the best thing to do was to sit back and do nothing. Knowing the season makes all the difference, doesn't it? We'd never plant crops in the depths of winter, so why do we try to do that in our own lives?"

To illustrate how each set of difficult circumstances has four stages or seasons, a "tough-times story" might go like this:

The Beginning (Autumn). At forty-five, Jane has a routine breast examination, and the doctor notices a lump. Mammogram, MRIs, and biopsies diagnose a malignant tumor. Jane realizes she has cancer and needs surgery.

The Dark Passage (Winter). Jane endures multiple surgeries, six weeks of chemotherapy, and months of radiation. She is exhausted and nauseated. A doctor suspects more cancer, and Jane feels like she can't endure another procedure. Loved ones that Jane assumed would show up do not. She wonders if she will survive to see her daughter graduate from high school.

Adaptation (Spring). Finally, the therapies end. Jane is deemed cancer-free and realizes that she has drawn support from new and surprising sources. She describes how living for today, with people who respect her as she now cares for herself, is her new highest priority. "Nobody escapes alive," she says, "so how can I live until I am dead?"

Return to Stability (Summer). As Jane's hair grows back and strength returns, she reaches out to deepen nurturing friendships. She plans her dream trip to Asia, and recognizing that her marriage isn't functional, she enters counseling.

Another tough-times story might go like this:

The Beginning (Autumn). Joe is a young, vibrant, software company president who finds that his business growth strategy is contrary to that of the board of directors. The founders also find Joe's ideas threatening, and after months of struggle, they ask him to leave. Joe struggles with the concept of "being fired" and looking for a job in a down economy. How can this be fair when his approach would have saved the company, which goes bankrupt the following year?

The Dark Passage (Winter). Joe looks for a job. Headhunters send him from interview to interview, yet nothing fits. He begins to doubt his skills and worries about his waning finances and moving his children, and if he'll ever be successful again. He and his wife fight daily. Weeks turn into months of unemployment. A foreclosure notice for their home arrives.

Adaptation (Spring). An old business associate calls out of the blue to check in. The ensuing conversation reminds Joe of past successes and what he loved about leading an organization. The friend suggests a meeting with his CEO. Inspired, Joe decides to look for work whether he's paid or not. He volunteers to head a transportation task force to investigate building a light rail system in his town.

Return to Stability (Summer). While Joe runs the task force, he meets community leaders who are impressed with his superior skills. Through these contacts, Joe is asked to run an exciting, nonprofit, clean-energy company and begins to build it from the ground up.

Equating the four stages of tough times to the seasons, we start with Autumn, because this is when things begin to "fall" apart. Leaves break away from the trees, and plants freeze and die. The seasons change and that which had fed us ends; like a marriage, a friendship, or good health. We watch it whither, and although we hope that we can find a way to make it last, no amount of vigilance will stave off this shift. We are called to take stock of our situation, ask questions, and gather information on what is changing to better adapt. Our natural reactions include denying changes and striking out in anger at those around us.

> *Every problem has in it the seeds of its own solution.*
>
> —NORMAN VINCENT PEALE

Winter, or the messy middle of tough times, comes next. It seems impossible that anything new will grow again. This phase is bleak, inhospitable, and can be depressing. It is always darkest before the dawn, when no solution is in sight. We feel helpless and hopeless.

If we can wait out Winter, Spring comes with a promise of new beginnings. We begin to see new possibilities. It is time to till the soil, decide what to plant, and get ready for the growing season. If we are courageous enough, we plant new seeds and do the work to create a garden that can feed us (for example, we work to create a new relationship, job, or home). This is a time of excitement, and as we consider the possibilities, we may feel overwhelmed.

In Summer, we care for our new seedlings, get rid of weeds that block their progress, and nurture our new plants to get back to a productive place. We must garner our courage and step out in new ways.

Wouldn't it be great if I could tell you that each season of tough times takes approximately two days? Just grin and bear it, and in eight days, everything will be all better! We know that it doesn't work like that. Mr. Tough Times has his own schedule, and he drives a pace car you won't be able to pass in this race. Some challenges will last weeks or months, while we must endure others for years.

For each set of tough times, there appears to be a total minimum suffering period. With a death of a grandparent, it might be six months before you find your footing.

> *In my own experience, the period of greatest gain in knowledge and experience is the most difficult period in one's life.... Through a difficult period, you can learn, you can develop inner strength, determination, and courage to face the problem.*
>
> —HIS HOLINESS THE DALAI LAMA

To adjust to a divorce, you may need at least three years. Not acting appropriately may mean that you extend your difficult-circumstances sentence. It helps to remember that there is a time to sow and a time to reap.

Getting scared makes things worse. You may focus only on surviving, which makes you ignore the bigger picture. Brain research shows that fear makes it easy to stay stuck in a particular stage, and it makes us lash out. For example, after a friend learned of a poor EKG result, I watched her ignore the information and then yell at the doctor and her spouse who brought it up. The problem didn't go away, just the doctor.

Having a map and a guidebook relaxes me when I'm in strange country, and it can help us relax if we know where we stand in the journey of tough times. Figuring out our "season" and what it entails helps us to map our next actions. Knowing my season, I can ask these questions:

- Is it time to ask questions?
- Is it time to stop?
- Is it time to brainstorm?
- Is it time to act?

In other words, I figure out if it is time to:

- Take stock
- Rest
- Sow new seeds
- Pull weeds

Sound easy? Here's the rub. We live in an action-focused culture. In the Western world, when things are not going our way, we are told to "get back to work," even when it might be time to rest. This four-phased approach may sometimes feel counterintuitive. On the other hand, if we are taught to go with the seasonal flow, it is a much easier ride. The rest of this book is divided into the four seasons. The beginning of each section will explain how to achieve the following:

- Tap your emotions to determine your current season.
- Recognize if you are stuck.
- Make it to the end.

The journey through the four stages has no set time limit. You can spend a day in one stage only to spend years in another. Some people never leave a stage and choose not to reengage: for example, the loss of a child may mire parents in the depths of winter for the rest of their days. However, you may suddenly move past a terrible heartache and, to your surprise, learn to love and laugh again.

Summary of the Four Stages

Stage	Season	Characteristics	Typical emotions	What to do	Check out chapter
Disruption	Autumn	Change	Denial and shock	Gather information	2 & 3
Messy Middle	Winter	Dark	Hopelessness and confusion	Slow down and let go	4 & 5
Adaptation	Spring	New possibilities	Optimism and overwhelmed	Be open	6 & 7
Stability	Summer	More solid ground	Relief and anxiety	Act with courage	8

Autumn

The art of progress is to preserve order amid change and to preserve change amid order.

—ALFRED NORTH WHITEHEAD

Overview

"Everything was going along fine, and then..." could be the alternate title for this first phase. When tough times appear, you might end that sentence with one of the following:

- ...the police called.
- ...we fought for the last time.
- ...our controller was charged with fraud.
- ...I went to the doctor.
- ...the market crashed.

> *Travelers, there is no path, paths are made by walking.*
>
> —ANTONIO MACHADO

The stability you enjoyed becomes a distant memory as you receive news that changes your reality. "Shift Happens" would be another good title. Things begin to fall apart.

How Are You Feeling? Shock and Denial

In the beginning of the biblical book of Job, after losing his children and livelihood, Job appears to downplay his predicament. "It is the will of God," he says. "All will be well." He attempts to stay on top of the game, to hold onto old beliefs, and to hope that everything will head quickly back to normal. In the tale, he seems embarrassed and worried that he's brought this mess upon himself.

I know that strategy. When I learned at forty that I had basal cell carcinoma (a nonlethal but serious form of skin cancer) on the end of my nose, I felt like a loser. I didn't want to tell people about it. It felt like I had failed. Did I not manage stress well, or was I too lax on sunscreen? What was wrong *with me* that I was in this situation? Would others judge me as damaged, weak, or pitiful? If I could have kept the skin cancer secret, I would have. I tried to pretend that it was no big deal and not think about it.

How We Get Stuck

Many societies acknowledge two physical death dates. In the Spanish Vaqueiro culture, we begin to die the day we lose our *gracia*, or spirit to live. The second death date is the actual end of life. In the Hindu culture, the first date of death is when a person expires, but the real death is considered the cremation ceremony (more graphically, it is when the skull cracks open on the funeral pyre as the soul escapes). In Borneo, the Dayak create a temporary burial site for a corpse until that second date of death, when the spirit has left and the body can be permanently buried. In culture after culture, there is *dead* and then there is *really dead*.

The transitional period between the two physical death dates is seen as risky for everyone involved. Many mourners make helping a loved one move from dead to really dead a high priority, because they believe that if the transitional soul gets stuck in between, he or she will wreak havoc—haunting the living, creating misfortune, or creating more death. Around the world, transitional souls believed to be traveling between the first and second deaths are perceived as deserving of pity and as potentially dangerous.

This common belief in two death dates seems like an interesting cross-cultural fact until you think of those in your everyday life who never move from getting bad news (a first ending or death date) to accepting their situation and working to adjust (the second date). Perhaps a friend refuses to accept the end of a marriage long after the divorce. How about those parents who undermine their children so that they won't leave the nest? Do you know someone who at fifty keeps trying to pretend that he is eighteen years old? These souls can cause great disaster. They have topics that can't be discussed ("Don't bring up Jim's drug addiction") and require others to walk on eggshells and pretend that there is no problem. Until we are willing to accept bad news, we are deserving of pity and potentially dangerous. It is in everyone's interest to look squarely at our circumstances and accept our lot.

In my case, I tried to delude myself that the carcinoma would go away or that my immune system would fight it off. I perceived myself young and healthy. The words "skin cancer" were incongruent with my self-assessment. Instead of researching treatment options and getting support from others, I tried to ignore the situation by reading novels and losing myself in the Internet. I sadly also ignored advice from family and friends to investigate different treatment options, and I pushed away potential support.

How to Make It Through: Gather Information

In transition, ask questions such as these:

- Where am I now?
- What have I lost?
- What are my resources, and who is with me?

Think of yourself as a general stepping on your own battlefield. Using an analogy from a three-thousand-year-old Chinese text by Sun Tzu, *The Art of War*, be that sage commander who before a battle, evaluates who he is fighting, the strength of his troops, who his allies are, and how best to approach his opponents. Determine who or what you are facing and your next best step.

When you have been shocked by a life crisis, asking these questions can be too much to handle at first. It's natural to be overwhelmed when a traumatic event occurs. Jerry White, founder of Landmine Survivors Network and Survivor Corps, describes this experience as "a loss of control or connection. Life has betrayed us." Our minds cannot wrap around the situation.

Jerry lost his leg to a landmine while hiking in Israel. He believes that the first step in recovering from a traumatic event is to "face the facts." He says, "Facing the facts is so hard because it demands that we come to grips with our worst fears. . . . Most of us would prefer to look away and carry on our merry way without thinking about these things, but without a closer look in the mirror, examining the wrinkles of our traumatized life, we can't make sound decisions, and then proceed to change and grow."

If we are terrified or traumatized, it's hard to ask data-gathering questions. My skin cancer panic kept me from having a clear understanding of the removal process, which then caused me even more distress when what I assumed would be a quick procedure became three multi-hour surgeries. There were easier, more-desirable treatment options, but because of my denial, I was at the mercy of what the first doctor prescribed. A lasting scar is my constant reminder of this painful lesson learned.

If you can't gather the necessary information, ask your friends and family to help you collect data. Get someone to accompany you to the doctor's office or to a meeting. Ask others to tell you what they see.

In the twenty years after writing *When Bad Things Happen to Good People*, Rabbi Harold Kushner asked his audiences during hundreds of lectures what helped them emerge after tragic circumstances. Again and again, he heard the same answer: community. Whether it's a trip to a doctor's office or the long walk through divorce proceedings, choosing the right companions through tough times will improve your capacity for taking stock in difficult circumstances and eventually arriving home unscathed.

> *We can only be said to be alive in those moments when our hearts are conscious of our treasures.*
>
> —THORNTON WILDER

CHAPTER 2

Get a Team

You cannot hope to build a better world without improving the individuals. To that end each of us must work for his own improvement, and at the same time, share a general responsibility for all humanity, our particular duty being to aid those to whom we think we can be most useful.

—MARIE CURIE

Welcome to the Club

Tough times issue an invitation. "Congratulations," they seem to say, "you've just been invited to join the ____________ Club," filling in the blank with one of the following:

- Lost a Parent
- Child of Divorce
- Been Fired
- Major Accident
- Bankruptcy

- Husband Had a Mistress
- Cancer
- Poverty
- Widowhood/Widowerhood

Tough times can be considered an initiation. You start out one place, and life pokes and prods you until you land in new territory. You start out in a marriage and eventually emerge as single, or you begin your career as a seasoned engineer and find yourself, four stages later, a neophyte teacher. Some initiations are smooth and others brutal.

If you go through a divorce, you are initiated into being single. If you have been fired, you join the Surviving Being Jobless Club. Traditionally, tough times are not experiences you would be expected to ever handle alone. For example, during initiation rites into manhood within the indigenous cultures of Africa or the Americas, caring community members monitor you from the sidelines; fellow initiates keep you company; and knowledgeable guides help you navigate. In the long-lasting world cultures, initiations or transitions from one societal role to another are not fully solitary.

The American pull-yourself-up-by-your-bootstraps attitude is not an advisable approach to confronting tough times. The state of Montana has one of the highest suicide rates in the country, and this has been attributed in part to an overly independent attitude. In the classic *Rites of*

Passage, Solon Kimbala suggests that "one dimension of mental illness may arise because an increasing number of individuals are forced to accomplish their transitions alone and with private symbols." Longevity studies continue to point to a *healthy, interdependent community* as a leading factor of health.

> *What should young people do with their lives today? Many things, obviously. But the most daring thing is to create stable communities in which the terrible disease of loneliness can be cured.*
>
> —KURT VONNEGUT JR.

During times of major loss, you would not be expected to grieve alone in many cultures. Around the world, people are expected to stop by and check on the mourners. In the United States, therapist and author Sally Babcock lost her adult son in an ice-skating accident in 2000. When I asked her how she survived such an extraordinary loss, she said, "For thirty days, friends and family visited us each evening, bringing food for dinner. Each would thankfully stay and allow me to talk about our son's passing over and over again. Combined with joining The Compassionate Friends [an organization that supports parents who have lost children], that's how I survived." The same expectation of support should be accorded for any major loss.

Your community can support you from three positions. First, you have *fellow travelers*. While sharing a common experience, you can exchange notes to track your progress. These folks remind you that you aren't crazy or weak when you hit road bumps similar to theirs. You can cheer each other along or laugh at the ridiculous predicaments you find yourselves in (like a jobless friend at a dinner party being asked, "So, how's work?").

Think of choosing your fellow traveling companions as you would when embarking on an extended trip, either abroad or through the wilderness. When I ask workshop participants or clients about the attributes of a good fellow traveler through tough times, I hear responses like these:

- Has a positive attitude
- Doesn't whine
- Can stand on her own two feet
- Won't quit
- Brings complementary skills
- Knows how to cook (I love that one)
- Is "low maintenance"

Second, there are those who root for you from the sidelines. When you have inadvertently joined the Health Crisis Club or the Lost a Parent Society, if I am not a member, I can't begin to understand the club's rites or support you as a fellow traveler. However, I can show up as a *caring community member*. In this role, I can provide comfort. I can remind you that you matter and that we hope you'll recover from the loss. I can cheer for your progress. Think about what makes for a great cheerleader or a fan in a stadium. A caring community member:

- Shows up
- Cheers with encouragement
- Is a loyal supporter of your personal best
- Doesn't yell advice from the sidelines (that's the coach's job)

> *A man's growth is seen in the successive choirs of his friends. For every friend he loses for truth he gains a better.*
>
> —RALPH WALDO EMERSON

You'll also want to include on your team *guides* who understand the tough times process. In indigenous cultures, elders or shamans accept this role. In a Western setting, you might look to a wise counselor, coach, or friend who was seasoned by completing a similar journey. It might be a sponsor in Al-Anon or Alcoholics Anonymous. Guides are expected to do the following:

- Provide appropriate advice
- Explain what to expect along the way
- Watch for danger signs that you are really stuck
- Push for your highest and best performance

Piece together a three-pronged support structure by (1) seeking out others in your position, (2) alerting family members and friends of your struggles, and (3) meeting with a therapist, coach, or spiritual counselor. Support groups like Alcoholics Anonymous, Al-Anon, and The Compassionate Friends are structured to provide all three forms of support. The Young Presidents' Organization, Heartland Circle, and other business groups that include confidential dialogue can serve as professional support structures, bringing together associates with similar experience, supporters, and subject area experts.

I also suggest four key team-member attributes for anyone, be it a fellow traveler, community member, or guide:

1. Doesn't try to "fix" you

> *I always felt that the great high privilege, relief, and comfort of friendship was that one had to explain nothing.*
>
> —KATHERINE MANSFIELD

The general support team role is to keep an initiate *relatively* safe while going through an induction ritual, be it into adulthood or into a new existence after a great loss. Elders know that it may be terrifying or terrible for the initiate, but their role is simply to ensure that the rite is completed. If it is not an end-of-life ritual, guides usually watch that the person is not irreparably harmed in the process. They know that there are "points of no return" and keep the initiate away from those edges. Otherwise, the candidates are left to conquer the struggle, and some suffering is seen as a necessary part of the growth process.

"Rescuing" another from an initiation would derail a rite of passage. It would not only set back the initiate but also endanger the community's health. After raising two boys into adulthood, I can understand why no one would want to thwart an initiation to manhood. In many cultures, the community indirectly watches over an initiate and lets him do the necessary work so that he can emerge in a new form, be it as an adult, a widow, or a community leader. We can see our role as encouraging the initiate's progress and reminding him that he is not abandoned in his struggles.

When I am in the darkest sections of tough times, I find it taxing to interact with people who are bothered by my suffering and want to "fix" me. I am bothered by their desire to offer quick advice or diminish my woes. I tell them "I'm fine" and avoid deep conversation.

I actually am a "recovering rescuer." Speaking from experience, trying to solve another's problems is rarely effective. I have found that by not allowing another his feelings and struggles, I can inadvertently worsen his suffering and slow his progress.

During her lifetime, Elisabeth Kübler-Ross conducted hundreds of workshops on how to support others through their grief. She set a clear rule in each session that when another is externalizing anger or sadness, he or she is not to be touched. She wrote, "It is important for us to teach the group not to touch others when they are into feelings, as this just puts a Band-Aid on their pain, implicitly or explicitly conveying the message: don't cry, it's going to be all right.... Once the bucket of repressed tears, anguish and anger has been emptied, one can correlate and evaluate one's behavior and replace the energy-draining with more positive attitudes and responses."

2. Supports Only Progress

> *I am speaking now of the highest duty we owe our friends, the noblest, the most sacred—that of keeping their own nobleness, goodness, pure and incorrupt.*
>
> —HARRIET BEECHER STOWE

In any of these team roles—fellow traveler, community member, or guide—we want to support the initiate to *complete* the journey. When we notice someone getting stuck, it's fair to call out what we see. There is a balance between compassionately listening to the person vent her frustrations and sharing direct feedback when it appears that she is mired.

Jane called from Massachusetts to say that she just attended a funeral of a friend's niece, who was brutally murdered by an ex-boyfriend. Jane wanted to tell me about the heart-wrenching eulogy given by the deceased's mother. Jane said, "She stood in front of a packed church and described how she had spent the week underneath twelve pillows, screaming in rage and howling in pain. Deedee, I could hardly stand to hear her express that level of suffering.

> *Trouble creates a capacity to handle it....Meet it as a friend, for you'll see a lot of it and had better be on speaking terms with it.*
>
> —OLIVER WENDELL HOLMES JR.

"The mother couldn't pull herself together enough to go to the viewing, and everyone was wondering if she would make it to the funeral. She said that the reason she was there was that a dear friend had arrived in her bedroom that morning and said, 'Millie, today we are going to stand up and practice getting dressed.' She then shared that today she knew she was going to survive the horror and that her friend had made it so." Jane said, "I think that's what we would do for each other." I would agree.

Recovering from loss seems to depend on our temperament, degree of attachment, and imposed cultural rules. For example, it would not be considered strange for an Egyptian woman to be mired in grief seven years after losing a child, but a traditional Balinese who laughs off a loved one's death would be within the standards of the culture. We cannot impose our own values on what someone is "supposed" to do in a difficult situation.

However, gentle nudges (like those that Millie's friend gave her) can be valuable support as we are moving through tough times. She wasn't asking her to stop mourning: it was just time to practice walking and getting dressed. I bet that Millie's friend knew in her bones that Millie needed to attend that funeral to hasten her healing. Her actions said, "I'm here, and you have what it takes to recover."

3. Can Bear Witness

> *Presence is a noun, not a verb; it is a state of being, not doing. States of being are not highly valued in a culture that places a high priority on doing. Yet, true presence, or "being with" another person carries with it a silent power—to bear witness to a passage, to help carry an emotional burden, or to begin a healing process.*
>
> —DEBBIE HALL

I gravitate to those who are not afraid of strong emotions. They provide comfort by being fully attentive and listening to me when I am sad or raging mad. These brave souls comfortably stick with the emotional storm, because they have ventured through the same dark waters that I am navigating. I am not required to be anywhere different from just where I am, which creates the space for me to move. This skill is often referred to as "bearing witness."

At the end of teaching a week-long doctoral class in New York City, I was pulled aside by one of my students, Claire, who quietly asked, "What do you think it means to bear witness?" Given the discretion of her questioning,

> *Those who do not know how to weep with their whole heart don't know how to laugh either.*
>
> —GOLDA MEIR

and to buy myself some more time to craft a teacher-worthy answer, I said, "Why do you ask?" She related a story that became impossible to forget.

She said, "Before this course, the last time I visited New York City was in September of 2001. I was staying in a hotel in the financial district on an upper floor. On the morning of the eleventh, I was in my room, getting ready to go out for the day, when I heard glass breaking and the sounds of destruction coming from outside. I ran to the window and could see that something had happened to one of the World Trade Towers. I stood at my window in shock. I didn't know what else to do.

"I don't want to tell you all that I saw, but I watched. I watched people jump, many people. I wouldn't let myself turn away because somehow I felt that it was important that I watched them fall, really saw them and prayed for them. It felt like the only thing I could do."

"Yours is the best description I have ever heard for bearing witness," I said. Our conversation turned to how she might continue in the role of bearing witness and sharing it with others. Her courage and fortitude modeled what is needed when another is suffering through tough times.

4. Find Someone Who Will Stand at the First Gate

> *Lots of people want to ride with you in the limo, but what you want is someone who will take the bus with you when the limo breaks down.*
>
> —OPRAH WINFREY

In the Sumerian myth included at the end of this book, the goddess Inanna, the Queen of Heaven and Earth, must pass through seven gates and give her crown, robes, and jewelry to the gatekeepers to reach the Underworld. Before the queen ventures forth, she requests a favor of her loyal servant, Ninshibur. "Wait for me here at the first gate, yet don't follow me underneath the earth. If I don't return after three days and three nights, go ask the gods to rescue me."

This decision reflects two key cross-cultural responsibilities during tough times. First, alert someone that you are struggling, and second, realize that you may need others to get you out if you are down too long.

Researcher Uwe P. Gielen explains that within traditional Tibetan communities, each villager belongs to a *phaspun* or "group of households whose members help each other during crisis situations." When a family member is dying, "it becomes incumbent upon his lama or spiritual guide, the monks of a nearby monastery, other members of his family's *phaspun,* the local *önpo* (astrologer), and various family friends to provide the family with emotional and material support."

Once alerted that you are suffering, your faithful servant will want to pay attention. Checking in by phone or bringing by a book or food allows her to gauge your progress. Setting up weekly or monthly appointments with a knowledgeable therapist or coach will ensure that you have someone standing at that gate. Attending a meeting of fellow travelers, such as The Compassionate Friends or a church group, is another way.

Psychiatrist Gerald G. May, author of *The Dark Night of the Soul*, speaks to the difference between clinical depression and the healing sadness that comes with darkness of tough times. "[A] person's sense of humor, general effectiveness, and compassion for others are not usually impaired in the dark night as they are in depression. There is also often a sense that down deep, people wouldn't really trade their experience of the dark night for more pleasure—it's as if they sense the rightness of it.... The signs of clinical depression are becoming well known these days and are generally recognizable in oneself or others if time is taken to consider them."

The Diagnostic and Statistical Model of Mental Health, or DSM IV, provides the following psychological definition for a major depressive episode:

A. Five (or more) of the following symptoms have been present during the same 2-week period and represent a change from previous functioning; at least one of the symptoms is either (1) depressed mood or (2) loss of interest or pleasure.

Note: Do not include symptoms that are clearly due to a general medical condition, or mood-incongruent delusions or hallucinations.

- depressed mood most of the day, nearly every day, as indicated by either subjective report (e.g., feels sad or empty) or observation made by others (e.g., appears tearful). Note: In children and adolescents, can be irritable mood.
- markedly diminished interest or pleasure in all, or almost all, activities most of the day, nearly every day (as indicated by either subjective report or observation made by others)
- significant weight loss when not dieting or weight gain (e.g., a change of more than 5% of body weight in a month), a decrease or increase in appetite nearly every day. Note: In children, consider failure to make weight gains.

- insomnia or hypersomnia nearly every day
- psychomotor agitation or retardation nearly every day (observable by others, not merely subjective feeling of restlessness or being slowed down)
- fatigue or loss of energy nearly every day
- feelings of worthlessness or inappropriate guilt (which may be delusional) nearly every day (not merely self-reproach or guilt about being sick)
- diminished ability to think or concentrate, or indecisiveness, nearly every day (either by subjective account or as observed by others)
- recurrent thoughts of death (not just fear of dying), recurrent suicidal ideation without a specific plan, or a suicide attempt or a specific plan for committing suicide

B. The symptoms do not meet criteria for a Mixed Episode.

C. The symptoms cause clinically significant distress or impairment in social, occupational, or other important areas of functioning.

D. The symptoms are not due to the direct physiological effects of a substance (e.g., a drug of abuse, a medication) or a general medical condition (e.g., hypothyroidism).

E. The symptoms are not better accounted for by Bereavement, i.e., after the loss of a loved one, the symptoms persist for longer than 2 months or are characterized by marked functional impairment, morbid preoccupation with worthlessness, suicidal ideation, psychotic symptoms, or psychomotor retardation.

The DSM IV appears to acknowledge that as we recover from difficulties, our symptoms will look very similar to clinical depression, yet there is a difference. We *need* to feel flat, sad, or exhausted as we travel the path through tough times.

If we sink too deeply into the Underworld, like Inanna, we may require help to bring us back. After years of working with clients and studying the dark night/tough-times journey, May believes that if medication is required to get back to the surface, it does not interfere "with deeper spiritual processes." Quoting author Judith Hooper, May says, "Before enlightenment, take Prozac and talk to your shrink. After enlightenment, take Prozac and talk to your shrink."

When we are asked to stand at the first gate, we don't follow another down into the Underworld. As caring community members, we are to pay attention and to offer any information we might have on the guideposts ahead. At the first gate, we are to watch whether we'll need to call someone in to rescue the traveler. Where we would have alerted tribal elders about danger signs in an initiatory process, we now look to health care professionals and therapists to identify the edges and pull someone out. If you suspect that someone is suffering from a clinical depression or can't recover from loss, seek professional expertise.

Kate shared her story of standing at the first gate. "One of my dearest friends committed suicide last fall. She left two children, ages nine and twelve. The day she died, the eldest son locked himself in his room and wouldn't come out. After a few hours, worried, I wrote a note saying, 'Are you okay in there? Just let me know.' He responded, 'I'm okay.' I then wrote the names of all the people who had gathered in the house that evening who loved him, so he would know that we were all there holding him, and slipped it back under the door. He eventually unlocked the door.

"Six months later, his father needed to go on a trip. I kept an eye on the kids during the week that he was away. Although his grandparents were taking a turn staying at the house, I received a surprise call from my twelve-year-old friend, who asked if I might be coming by the house. All plans were tossed away, and I said I would. That night, I spent the evening watching him do homework and just being near him. That's the first time he's called me, although I call and visit him often."

Summary

During tough times, you should have three types of support at your side:

1. *Fellow travelers* who are committed to getting to the other side.
2. *Caring community members* who
   - Provide comfort
   - Listen and bear witness
   - Do not rescue you (only you can do that)
   - Support progress
3. A *guide* who understands the journey that you are confronting and
   - Tells you where you are
   - Watches for warning signs
   - Provides pointers along the way

When in doubt about your future, get a team. Difficult experiences hold opportunity and learning. There will be times when we need to restructure our finances, get out of bad marriages or find new work. As your life shifts, share it with someone. Look for another who can relate to your travails and travel with you. Find those who can keep an eye on your progress and overall health. Call on those who will let you embark into unknown territory, but will watch that you don't get dangerously lost.

As we will now explore, you can trick yourself into asking important questions during the Autumn phase not only by enlisting a community but also by adopting a hopeful attitude and practicing gratitude. All around the world, we are told to count blessings each day. Some are told to notice what they appreciate each morning or are expected to pray with appreciation five times a day, as in the Islamic tradition. Seeing disaster as holding potential opportunity decreases fear and moves the brain into a more learning-centered attitude.

CHAPTER 3

Believe in a Happy Ending

Become a student of change. It is the only thing that will remain constant.

—ANTHONY J. D'ANGELO

Things Might Get Better...or They Might Not

Eighteen women gathered one cold January weekend for a "Thriving through Tough Times" workshop. It was not the lightest topic yet one that elicited lots of shared laughter from the group. They ranged in age from twenty-nine to timeless grandmas, and everyone had valuable advice to contribute. When we spoke about what to do when we land in difficult circumstances, one of the group elders wryly added, "When times get tough, I tell myself, 'Things might get better [long pause] or they might not.'"

The grounded optimism of these words summed up the workshop theme. Many of these women had overcome some very tough times. They had learned from their experiences and garnered great opportunities as a result. Many modeled how life can indeed improve through adversity, yet they were realistic: when you lose a child or your best friend, things might not get better, but some good can appear in the future. It's worth sticking around to see what's next.

The French philosopher Blaise Pascal posed a famous wager. He suggested that we should believe in a joyful afterlife because if there were nothing out there waiting for us, there would be no harm done. Regardless of the outcome, we will live until then with greater happiness. In this wager, I find the underlying truth of "things might get better...or they might not."

We can apply the essence of this wager found in ancient wisdom and modern psychology to our "little deaths," as Buddhism describes tough times. A job/marriage/situation ends or "dies," and we enter into a dark time of transition. If things get better (or not), a new career/relationship/life emerges. In many spiritual traditions, little deaths are seen as valuable practices to prepare us for the big one at our physical end.

Although we are promised insight if we survive tough times, we are not ensured that we will love this next life more than our last. Rabbi Howard Kushner speaks of how losing his teenage son to a rare illness made him spiral deep into a fight with God, testing his faith to an extreme. When he emerged, he said, "I am a more sensitive person, a more effective pastor, a more sympathetic counselor because of Aaron's life and death than I would ever have been without it. And I would give up all of those gains in a second if I could have my son back."

Applying Pascal's optimistic challenge to life's endings and new beginnings can facilitate your journey through tough times. Positive psychologist Dr. Dan Baker explains in his book *What Happy People Know* that those who are able to look on difficult situations with optimistic beliefs are much more apt to live longer and more richly.

> *Let us weigh the gain and the loss of calling heads that God exists. Let us assess the two cases. If you gain, you gain all; if you lose, you lose nothing.*
>
> —BLAISE PASCAL

Around the world, we are counseled to be calm and focused on the path ahead, whether meeting a little or a big ending. To calm ourselves through transition, we are counseled to repeat a prayer or saying to visualize a positive future. Brain researchers agree that favorite positive phrases can both calm and prepare us for whatever adventure is ahead.

A *mantra* is a sound, word, or phrase that is repeated to aid in concentration or meditation. Derived from Sanskrit, *mantra* means "instrument of thought" or "man-think."

Around the world, people repeat phrases to aid transition, such as the prayer of the mystic Julian of Norwich "All shall be well, and all shall be well, and all manner of things shall be well," when they are afraid or distraught.

We also chant prayers or mantras to comfort the dying, reminding them of the life to come. Many cultures strive for a "good death" or one that is conscious and peaceful, often because the members believe this will support getting to the best "next destination" possible. In the Catholic tradition, the prayer "Hail Mary...pray for us sinners now and at the hour of our death" is repeated, while Hindus sing devotional prayers and chant Vedic mantras throughout the process. As Gandhi died, he uttered the divine name Sri Ram again and again.

Mantras are my verbal opening bow to my opponent, Mr. Tough Times. Employing martial arts and conflict-resolution strategies, I think of difficult circumstances as a respected adversary. "Stepping onto the mat" with my opponent when he appears, I repeat silently,

- "Good teacher." I borrow the martial arts belief that our opponents are our best instructors. I am reminded that I can learn something and become wiser—a big personal selling point.
- "Opportunity, lots of opportunity." Conflict always holds opportunity for things to get better.

- "I get to be here." This might be my only opportunity, in this body anyway, to have this experience.

Author and executive coach David Baum relied on the following passage from the Persian poet Jelaluddin Rumi when undergoing major bypass surgery in his early forties. Throughout the surgery preparations, and as he was wheeled into the operating room, he repeated, "Break my heart. Break it once again, so I can truly love."

You can set your mantras to music. Therapist and musician Shaun Phoenix composed a death chant as her mother was dying of dementia. This has now become Shaun's "song in travail":

> This is my letting go
> This is my surrender
> This is my letting go
> This is my surrender
> I am only spirit
> I am only light
> All else is illusion
> I return, I return, I return

While working through a divorce and her ex-husband's multiple sclerosis, Deborah also set her favorite saying to music. She repeated, "We give thanks for unknown blessings already on their way."

A workshop participant offered her father's favorite mantras: "Everything happens for a reason." Explaining how these words provide her solace and courage, she said, "By repeating this phrase, I accept my circumstances...then I figure I better start looking for that damn reason."

For me, "Everything happens for a reason" raises a counter-argument. As a silly example, I once put my favorite wool sweater in the dryer. It shrunk three sizes, making it impossible to wear. I loved that sweater, and I was angry with myself for not paying attention when I loaded the machine. This incident gave me the same feeling that I have about those perplexing experiences for which I can't see any possible reason. Why did I have to give up such a great piece of clothing? I had a sweater and then I didn't. I wanted to reverse time and catch a mistake.

The same week of the shrunken sweater, an acquaintance committed suicide almost exactly nine years after her husband had done the same. At her memorial service, watching their two young adult children suffering, I was at a loss. I had been told that it might have been a change of antidepressants that pushed this mother to kill herself. She was described at the funeral as being happy, vibrant, and fully involved in our community just months before. Knowing that bad

> *There is no one luckier than he who thinks himself so.*
>
> —GERMAN PROVERB

medical advice had potentially taken this life almost made this reality worse. It was like the sweater on a grand and terrible scale. Wasn't this another awful mistake?

Be it a sweater or an unjustifiable loss, I recognize that I may not fathom the reason for an issue, but there may still be one. As a wise Buddhist friend advises, "Knowing is the booby prize." Whether or not everything happens for a reason, holding the *attitude* that everything has a purpose is ubiquitous advice in the major spiritual traditions and can literally keep us alive during tough times.

"Everything happens for a reason" may be the guiding mantra for thriving through difficult circumstances. Austrian psychiatrist Victor Frankl wrote, "Man's search for meaning is the primary motivation in his life." In his seminal book whose first title was *Say Yes to Life in Spite of Everything*, Frankl describes three years as a prisoner in Auschwitz and two other locations. When prisoners lost a sense of meaning in the rightness of the larger situation, Frankl found that they would give up the fight to survive. They would smoke the last cigarette that they had carefully saved, curl into the fetal position, and soon die. In contrast, believing that there was a reason for what had occurred kept others alive against all odds.

Frankl himself was living proof. A prominent Jewish psychologist who could have escaped to America, he chose to stay behind with his mother, father, and wife after finding a scrap of the Torah on honoring one's parents.

For Frankl, remaining with his loved ones was an initial reason that he had become a prisoner, but in his darkest hours in the concentration camp, he began to lose hope that there was a purpose for the misery. On a particularly terrible day, with the threat of the gas chambers close, he was struck with a vision of being in a well-appointed conference room filled with colleagues. In fine clothes and comfort, he saw himself lecturing on his findings as a concentration camp survivor. As he returned to the present, the concentration camp became the ultimate learning laboratory on survival. All his experiences, both horrid and heart opening, then held meaning and the potential for growth. He believed that this kept him alive.

If we accept that everything happens for a reason, instead of asking, "Why me?" we move to "So now what will I do?" Kushner couldn't make sense out of why he had lost his son, but he realized that he always held the power to create a reason or make the experience meaningful. A bout with cancer can become an initiation into a deeper understanding of life's beauty and fragility. The loss of a job can open us to a new awareness of our core desires. A spouse leaving can be nurtured into a delicious relationship with our inner self. A suicide can rally heightened support for those who suffer from mental illness. We can create a meaning or a purpose. Like Frankl, we have the opportunity to turn our existence into a living laboratory.

As Dr. Rachel Naomi Remen reminds us, "Meaning is a form of strength. It has the power to transform experience, to open the most difficult of work to the dimension of joy and even gratitude. Meaning is the language of the soul." While we don't know if everything happens for a greater reason, we have the opportunity to make it true. We can thus believe that everything is innately right, that it is here for a purpose, and thus brings greater meaning into our lives.

Envision a Happy Ending

Delving deeper into mantras, I am reminded of a client named Betty who dissolved a business partnership that she had built seven years prior. It was a painful divorce of sorts in which she wanted out and her partners felt that she was needlessly abandoning them. After six months of negotiation and dividing clients and office furniture, Betty finally struck out on her own. When she shared her experiences during the transition, I had never seen her so stressed yet so resolved to move forward.

Once she was in a new office and working with people that she adored, I asked Betty what survival skills pulled her through those tough times. She said, "There were really bad days, when my partners angry with my leaving put up all sorts of roadblocks. Their wishes could easily get distracting and scary, so to save myself, I created a discipline before work each day. At the beginning of this mess, I wrote down a half dozen goals describing the future I wanted to create. Each morning, I would pull out my list and read it over. I centered on what really mattered. Then, when a new demand came from my ex-partners, I compared it to the list. Does their need to keep that file cabinet, for example, matter to me? With an exciting ending in mind, I was much better able to wade through the mess and emotions."

Betty essentially created a customized set of mantras that she repeated to herself each morning. She said, "I run a profitable business with happy employees and with people I enjoy and respect." These phrases invoked optimism, which allowed her to focus and approach her challenges creatively. The following exercise will help you build invigorating phrases to support you through the confusing middle stages of tough times. From a cross-cultural perspective, you will practice envisioning a positive afterlife that might make the pain worthwhile.

Envision an Exciting Future: Personalized Mantra Exercise

1. Find a quiet place where you can work undisturbed for a half-hour. Bring a notebook and pens.
2. Write down, without much consideration, the struggles that are capturing your attention. What

has brought you into tough times? Is it a relationship, a job, health? Write your list, bringing into your consciousness that which is not yet resolved. These are the objects of your inquiry during this exercise.

3. Seat yourself comfortably, and close your eyes, drawing in a few deep breaths to relax. Let all thoughts go.
4. Slowly open your eyes to read this step, and then close them to visualize the following. Around the world, it is believed that we can travel through time. Through our dreams, we can visit any of the many possible futures waiting for us. Vision quests and shamanic drumming journeys can also take us there, and we can travel out to see what awaits. See yourself traveling to "the best of all possible futures," where your struggles have been resolved. It might be a year from now, three years from now, or even tomorrow. Rest here, and see this place. Take it in.
5. Feel how you feel here. What colors and details do you see around you? With one foot in this place, softly open your eyes to jot down details.
6. Who is with you? If the object of your inquiry is a relationship, notice how that relationship is working. What is different? How does it feel? Gently

opening your eyes, not leaving this waking dream, add what you notice.

7. Notice your body. If your inquiry was around your physical nature, notice what is different and how it feels. Add any details.
8. What are you doing? Transport yourself to your work, whatever or wherever that is. Notice what you find. If you are inside, go to a window, and notice where you are. If you are outside, what might some of the details be?
9. What images, symbols, and surprises live in the best of all possible futures? Draw them if that helps you to flesh out what you found.
10. Open your eyes and reflect on what you found in the best of all possible futures. How would you describe it to others? What would it look like? What would be its highlights? Add these details to your notebook.
11. Now translate this vision into one to three phrases that will remind you where you are heading. The trick is to write these sayings as though the desired future is happening right now. Use present tense and positive language. "I have a great job doing what I love and am paid well," is an example (even if you are currently out of work or have a terrible, low-paying position).

To "fake it until you make it," repeat these sayings multiple times every day. Scientific research shows that we notice only what we are looking for. If you tell yourself that you have a great job, your mind will search for the conditions to make that so.

Summary

To employ our best problem-solving strategies, we want to create an enlivening vision for the future and remind ourselves of it each day.

- We can find phrases or mantras to calm and support us.
- We can hold a belief that there can be a happy ending, and allow our brain to search for a way to make it so.

You have now enlisted a team, and you have armed yourself with positive phrases or mantras to support you. The tough work of letting go of what you once enjoyed comes next. You may need to break old habits, say goodbye to loved ones, or leave behind old beliefs, possessions, or even parts of yourself. We now move from Autumn into Winter.

Winter

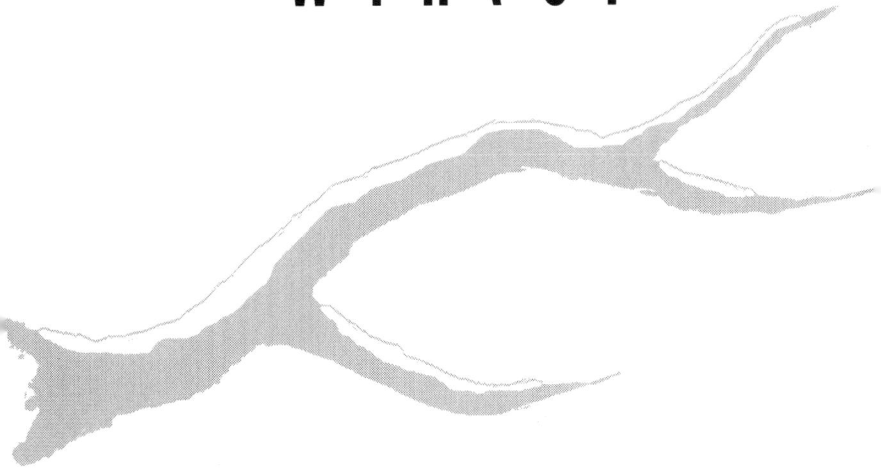

When we fall on the ground, it hurts us, but we also need to rely on the ground to get back up.

—KATHLEEN MCDONALD

Overview

When we reach the second phase of tough times, Winter, we recognize that things have officially fallen apart. Although we accept the ending, we can't make the tough times disappear. This is a chaotic period when we can't see a feasible solution. We know there's a mess but don't know how to fix it.

In the sixteenth century, the Spanish Christian mystic and poet John of the Cross was imprisoned for more than eight months for attempting to reform the Carmelite order. He described those wintery times in jail as a "dark night of the soul." Like John of the Cross, we can lose hope during this phase that a higher power exists. We may lose our faith that everything works out in the end, that the world is a good place or that others can be trusted.

Dark is the operative word for the second phase of tough times. We cope with bleak, disempowering emotions. It's impossible to see a workable future solution. The present is confusing and murky. Here's where "it's darkest before the dawn."

Planting new seeds in Winter is a bad idea. Ask any four-season farmer: winter is when you rest. It's the time you sharpen your tools. You slow down and take care of yourself and your home. You can't plow the fields, and planting seeds under snow would be silly and wasteful.

During the Winter of difficult conditions, trying to quickly create something new is counterproductive. You need to recover. You need to take stock of where you stand. Rushing around and using up your resources is foolish and can be dangerous, as you will exhaust what energy you have in a harsh, dark climate. Using Jane's example in Chapter 1, in the winter of cancer treatment, conserving energy is tantamount for survival. It would be a poor time to take on her marriage issues, let alone plan a trip or a new career.

After Winter, there will be a time to act. During a challenge's Spring and Summer, you want to be rested and ready to take risks, make phone calls, or do research. After a loss, you must be brave enough to wait through the uncertain, dark, confusing Winter, but then you must also be bold enough when the time comes to choose to try again.

How Are You Feeling? Sadness, Regret, Hopelessness and Rage

The Greeks gave us the image of this murky space being like the Underworld. It is as though we descend into a lightless cave or tunnel and lose our bearings. The Buddhists use the term *nothingness* to describe it, and medieval Christian mystics described it as the "negative path" where nothing is clear. All these traditions contend that we must visit Winter during major changes to be able to return to stability. It is considered critical that we fumble our way *through* the blackness to get to the other side. While valuable, it can be miserable.

Accepting loss, we move naturally into feelings of grief. These include the dark feelings of sadness, hopelessness, confusion, and sometimes rage. We play the "what if" game. "What if I hadn't left that meeting early? Would I still have gotten fired?" or "What if I hadn't smoked?" As in the Jewish mourning rituals, we want to tear at our clothing and are sometimes sickened by what is now gone. We suffer as we are pushed to let go.

How We Get Stuck

> *Old age, to the unlearned, is winter; to the learned, it's harvest time.*
>
> —YIDDISH SAYING

Philosophers and brain researchers liken how we perceive reality to watching a movie. Thousands of years ago, Plato, in his "Allegory of the Cave," portrayed humans as chained to chairs facing a cave wall where puppeteers projected the shadows of puppets from behind. When a shape passes in front of our eyes, we describe reality and tell each other "that is a dog" or "that is a tree," creating common agreement about the fuzzy images in front of our eyes. Evaluating our lives, we might say, "That's what a good marriage looks like" or "That's a healthy financial market."

When we see a truer picture of life, Plato noted, it can be both painful and difficult. We must release the old chains or beliefs. In the second stage, we realize that we've been deluding ourselves, but we still don't know how to get ourselves out of this lousy situation.

Say that I'm a heavy drinker and have been told if I don't stop drinking, I will die or my family will leave. To move past this stage, I have to let go of alcohol. Being stubborn and continuing to drink will not stop my relationships from ending or my health from being destroyed. If I'm stuck, I dig myself a deeper and darker pit.

> *The little reed, bending to the force of the wind, soon stood upright again when the storm had passed over.*
>
> —AESOP

The need to let go and mourn what we have lost doesn't go away just because we can avoid it. If we do not grieve, it will lie in wait for us and catch us unaware later. It becomes what we run from in the quiet moments. What we don't separate from, we continue to carry. In the African Dagara tradition, unprocessed grief is seen as an illness that can adversely affect the entire community: "Just as a wound on your leg cannot be approached as the leg's problem alone but must be treated as a problem for the entire body, a person in a village who is sick with grief sickens the rest of the village."

How to Make It Through: Recover and Practice Flexibility

> *All things arise,*
> *Suffer change,*
> *And pass away.*
> *This is their nature.*
> *When you know this,*
> *Nothing perturbs you,*
> *Nothing hurts you.*
> *You become still.*
> *It is easy.*
>
> —ASHTAVAKRA GITA 11:1

Westerners are not generally comfortable with this dark, wintry stage. We do our best to avoid it. We are encouraged to stay busy, fight for what we want, and be proactive. "Rise above it," we are counseled. While these are valuable skills in other phases, here quick action will stop us in our tracks. To make our way through this chaotic phase, we need to slow down, rest, recover, and stay flexible.

When we are in the depths of transition, we need a gentle approach. Traditions around the world associate this dark passage with water. To survive in the middle of any body of water, you need to conserve energy. Thrashing and pushing will only exhaust you and make drowning more likely. The standard advice in a riptide, for example, is to not resist and to wait until it releases its hold on you.

How can you rest, float, and go with the flow for a while? Allow yourself to recuperate from all the change you are undergoing. Exhaustion is also a good indicator that you are not being flexible or are hanging on needlessly. Is fighting to keep your husband in the marriage taking all your energy? Are you constantly tracking a child's substance abuse, waiting up each night to check her breath? If your old approaches are wearing you out, they need revision.

This is a time for *re*'s: *relax*, *recuperate*, *recover*, *rejuvenate*, *reflect*, and *reassess*. Don't start any new projects in Winter. Instead look for what should be left behind or at least left for another day. Lighten your load and carry only what will serve you in the future. The advice for Winter is to be flexible. *Be* as much as possible, and open to new and better solutions. See where you can let go of "doing," at least for now. Recover your strength for the exciting times ahead.

CHAPTER 4

Give Yourself a Break

And this is important to remember: given the fact of pain as a normal part of the experience of life, one may make the pain contribute to the soul, to the life meaning. One may be embittered, ground down by it, but one need not be. The pain of life may teach us to understand life and, in our understanding of life, to love life. To love life truly is to be whole in all one's parts; and to be whole in all one's parts is to be free and unafraid.

—HOWARD THURMAN

Tough times are often terrifying. When the ground on which we relied shifts and our basic safety feels under attack, panic kicks in, or we become immobilized, like deer in the headlights. From a physiological perspective, the amygdala in the center of the brain activates our survival reflexes. Adrenaline courses through our system. Awash in fear chemicals, we want to run, hit someone, or stare out the window like a zombie.

> *The deeper that sorrow carves into your being, the more joy you can contain.*
>
> —KAHLIL GIBRAN

This panicked state not only adversely affects our long-term health, but it restricts more complex abilities like creative problem solving and rational thought. The fear pushes us to react, and often stupidly. Witnessing others in this state, I have seen marriage-wounding attacks on a spouse for investing in the stock market, homes sold needlessly at fire-sale prices, and jobs quit at the worst possible time. None of these were ultimately good relationship or financial decisions.

World traditions provide calming techniques to bring us into more rational thinking during this in-between "messy middle" of tough times. The following tricks allow us to control the crazy fear-based reactions so that we can reactivate higher-reasoning brain functions and lower our anxiety and our blood pressure.

Take a Break

We don't recover well in high gear. Every culture I have studied advises a prescribed period where its members are required to sit and just "be with loss." The Jewish tradition of "sitting shiv'ah" for seven days is an example. A place is designated as a house of mourning. Mourners sit low to the floor and may not engage in any distractions (work, sex, dressing up, or looking at themselves in mirrors). Shoes are not to be worn. It is a time of thinking and prayer. The mourners are required to slow down and confront the situation.

In other traditions, mourners are required to observe all sorts of restrictions that set them apart and slow their ability to jump back into everyday life. Among the Olo Ngaju of Borneo, mourning periods and restrictions are set by the relationship a mourner has to the departed. Clear signals like diet and hair adornments symbolize that this person is not part of the social fabric during this time. Distant relatives are considered "impure" and set apart from the community for a few days, whereas the widow or widower is given additional restrictions and not allowed to remarry until a final ceremony in which the taboos are lifted.

Slowing down and setting oneself apart is counter-intuitive Western culture. When we slow down and pay attention, we feel the pain of the loss. I never would have slowed down to recover if I hadn't been forced to during some tough times. Being a runner from the age of seventeen, when sadness arose, I was able to literally run away from it. Endorphins kicked in, and I could keep soldiering on.

When I struggled through the "why me" conflict of skin cancer, I was awarded two weeks of rest, whether I wanted them or not. During a surgery to remove a basal cell carcinoma, I had skin removed from behind my ear, grafted to my nose, and held in place by what looked like a pincushion. I was counseled that skin grafts don't always "take." To help with the healing process, I was forbidden to increase my heart rate (absolutely no running) or position my face below my heart (no yoga, another favorite escape) for fourteen days. I didn't want to go out much because I looked like Pinocchio and felt like a bomb had gone off in my face. Other than a walk each day, I sat in my "house of mourning" while my children were off at school.

I cried for most of the time. I grieved for my face and the recent U.S. invasion of Iraq. In my sorrow, I also reflected on losses I had ignored or brushed away when they occurred. A well of sadness overflowed within me. I cried because I would never be young again and I was nearing the end of parenting as my son was heading off to high school that September. I grieved about how rarely I saw my sisters now that we were adults. Years of unprocessed grief welled to the surface. I pulled myself together, made dinner, and then cried more the next day. I was a basket case.

Looking back, those two weeks were a strange yet important gift. I faced feeling pain that I had ignored since

I was a child, and I survived it. I now can let others feel their own anguish, because I am less terrified of my own. I don't necessarily enjoy feeling emotional pain, but it is no longer a sort of dragon that I try to keep at bay. I am less controlled by my own pain management strategies.

My grieving process was far from complete, but I had allowed myself to go beneath the surface. I realized that I could go into it and would return. Over the next months, I spent quality time bobbing above and below the surface. Sadness and I became close partners as it painted a gray sheen on my life. Because I had learned about the chaos phase or messy middle of tough times through years of research, I knew that grief was a standard component of every tradition's spiritual journey. It came with the program and was sometimes "walking the land of the gray clouds." It didn't feel like a mental illness, just a period of suffering.

As Elisabeth Kübler-Ross explained, "As difficult as it is to endure, depression has elements that can be helpful in grief. It slows us down and allows us to take stock of the loss. It makes us rebuild ourselves from the ground up. It clears the deck for growth. It takes us to a deeper place in our soul that we would not normally explore."

It is true that, for some, chemical depression makes it impossible to come back without medical intervention. It is critical that your community watch for danger signs of long-term or debilitating depression. A skilled therapist on your team can support you during this time. Yet, my experience, and that of many others, shows that if we allow ourselves to go to this place of darkness, we return more authentic and stronger because of it.

My clients find periodic slowdown periods to be liberating. Although they are not initially thrilled with the idea of giving up numbing themselves for a time, the period becomes ultimately empowering. As one client said,

> At first, I didn't want to take your advice to take off a month after finishing a major project. I had no idea what I would do. When you would ask me, "What do you love to do?" other than "To be with my son," I had no answers. Not "doing" anything was uncomfortable and scared me, but as I adapted and spent time with myself, I remembered what I deeply valued. I love to paint and grieved how that had disappeared from my life. My son just became a teenager, and I have worked so hard over the past five years that I missed too much of his childhood. My month off pushed me to reorganize my life so I can have more time with my son and do the things I love. If I hadn't slowed down and taken stock of where I was, none of this would have happened.

Give Yourself a Year

In addition to slowing down, many cultures suggest that we give ourselves at least a year to recover from a major transition. The Islamic, Hindu, Jewish, and Christian religions, among others, advise a year-long mourning period when grieving parents or other close relatives. Until recently, Westerners were widely expected to dress differently and recite special prayers to remember that year of mourning. In the United States, elaborate mourning practices including black clothing or armbands and social restrictions lasted until the early twentieth century. Practicing Jews are expected to recite the Kaddish prayer at every appropriate service for twelve months after the death of a parent.

Around the world, in the Islamic tradition, older women are still expected to grieve for a year. North African women wear white during this time, while Middle Eastern women wear black and Turkish women subdued colors. With prescribed times for grieving, mourners get time to slow down and are also given a cultural break.

Translating this to tough times, the traditions seem to counsel, "Don't expect to get on top of a new routine until you've practiced it for at least twelve months." Allow yourself to be messy, confused, and in a learning mode. After a major loss, expect your birthday, New Year and cultural and religious holidays to be new experiences. You aren't expected to be part of daily activities. Depending on the culture, you may be given dispensation to grieve or to laugh inappropriately. Mourners are treated more gently and given the benefit of the doubt. It's a time to say yes to only those commitments that make you come alive; all else is to be left for another time.

During a year following any large shift, six months is my low point. This became clear when I entered parenthood. I noticed that my husband and I became discouraged about six months after the arrival of a child. After our first son, I remember thinking, "I should have lost all this baby fat by now," "We should be settled into this new family configuration," and "Why is this still so ridiculously hard?" Six months is a long time to endure the new chaos and confusion, and by then we have used up our just-muscle-it-through reserves.

As new parents, we thought, "If our culture's standard mourning or adjustment period historically is a year, shouldn't we be allowed the same?" We knocked off parts of our old life when each new baby arrived. The metaphoric gravestones could have read:

- Young Couple—RIP June 1989
- Family of Three —B: June 1989, D: March 1991
- Moving from man-to-man (two adults, two kids) into zone defense—June 1994

"It takes a year" has become my favorite piece of advice to any new parent. I selfishly enjoy seeing the relief it brings to a young mother's face. As an older, wiser mother once told me, "You are not supposed to be graceful when your children are young." For any major change, give yourself the same dispensation.

Welcome the Feelings

As Thomas Lewis, Fari Amini, and Richard Lannon describe in *A General Theory of Love*, when we bond with someone or something, the limbic system emits a pleasing blend of chemicals, including oxytocin. We like those chemicals and want to keep them coming. Think of the Labrador retriever outside the grocery store, howling for her human. If she could translate her brain signals into English, she might be saying, "I need the comforting presence of my master. I miss my oxytocin. Give me baaaaaack my oxytocin!" When we love someone or something, we attach ourselves to it. The resulting mother bear instinct is a fantastic, evolutionary feature that keeps our young alive.

Take away what I love, and I am going to be unhappy. I may get scared and angry. I may battle with sorrow and helplessness. I will feel pain, and because pain hurts, it is natural to avoid it. We try to run away from our feelings and get busy or numb out in hopes that they will go away.

The Buddhist and Hindu traditions are clear: having an aversion to what we don't like makes it worse. From the Christian tradition, we are told to "love our enemies," which can apply to unwelcome emotions like helplessness or grief. Confusion or sadness does not go away because we pretend it is not there. Pushing against or running away from our struggles will not cure them. In different cultures, we are counseled to notice and be with tough emotions when they appear. From the Islamic Sufi tradition, the poet Rumi suggests that we see our interior as a home where every emotion is welcomed as an honored guest. We invite everyone in, whether my buddy Joy or that strange character Insecurity. They visit and we keep an eye on them as we might if we were hosting a dinner party.

Remembering this, I have developed a habit of acknowledging awkward internal visitors with "Hello, Fear," or "Hi there, Frustration." By recognizing that I'm nervous, sad, miserable, or afraid, I calm down. When I don't resist the new arrival, both the emotion and I seem to ease. I have to giggle when I find myself saying, "Hi, Anxiety." Ain't that the truth at times! Recognizing that loss (including the loss of oxytocin) can be physically painful, we can acknowledge that discomfort with "Hello, Pain."

By welcoming feelings, we further accept our circumstances and make them conscious. "The job is gone, and

I am terrified and really sad," we might say. In admitting our circumstances externally and internally, we move beyond denial and resistance to better locate where we stand. Facing our situation is a healthy strategy for making progress through the four phases of tough times.

Look within. What emotion can you welcome right now?

Allow Anger

I appreciate the authenticity of the biblical character Job as he grieved. When his life falls apart he gets really pissed off. Screaming at God, he states his case about why it is unfair that he has been treated so poorly. He mourns the good he once had. His harangues go on for pages as he remembers in detail how rich, respected, and loved he once was and now just how horrid his life is. Translator Stephen Mitchell notes in *The Book of Job* how it appears that biblical scribes over the centuries have tried to fix what seemed like blasphemy by tweaking Job's words. Even

> *Don't cling to anything and don't reject anything. Let come what comes, and accommodate yourself to that, whatever it is. If good mental images arise, that is fine. If bad mental images arise, that is fine, too. Look on all of it as equal, and make yourself comfortable with whatever happens. Don't fight with what you experience, just observe it all mindfully.*
>
> —BHANTE HENEPOLA GUNARATANA

so, Job's rage at God shines through; he's livid and he doesn't care if God knows it.

Shortly before she passed away in 2004, Elisabeth Kübler-Ross brought together three decades of death and dying work in her book *On Grief and Grieving*. She provided concise guidance on why screaming like Job is essential: "Anger is a necessary stage of grief. Be willing to feel your anger, even though it may seem endless. The more you truly feel it, the more it will begin to dissipate and the more you will heal."

The power of anger rightfully scares us. People kill each other out of anger. They hit or verbally abuse their loved ones. However, feeling anger is different from using that passion to hurt another. Job doesn't strike his wife, insult his gathered friends, or kick his dog; he *externalizes* his anger.

Many cultures have ritualized the externalization of anger to move the process along. The Dagara tribe in Burkina Faso, Africa, uses communal water rituals to transform the anger, rage, frustration, and sadness of grief. An angry person is seen as someone "on the road to tears."

Anthropologist Renato Rosaldo spent thirty months among the Ilongot in the jungle northeast of Manila, Philippines. In 1972, he and his wife, Michelle, studied the Ilongot cultural practices, most salient of which was headhunting. When the Ilongot explained that the rage of grief impelled them to headhunt, Rosaldo didn't believe them. He writes, "My own inability to conceive the force of anger in grief led me to seek out another level of analysis that could provide a deeper explanation for older men's desire to headhunt."

Rosaldo's perspective completely changed when Michelle accidentally fell to her death during their time with the Ilongot. Overcome by the anger of his loss, Rosaldo finally understood how the ritual of headhunting provided the Ilongot men with relief. As they explained, they tossed away the head of the victim along with their rage. Although Rosaldo did not partake in this ritual, he understood the need to acknowledge and find a culturally accepted outlet to externalize the sometimes extraordinary rage that comes with grief.

Rage is scary. It frightens me when I see it in others and in myself. I suspect that heartless torture and murders around the globe are borne of grief's rage. I find these brutal acts too similar to the classic Greek author Homer's description of mourning's wrath to interpret them as simply evil. In *The Iliad*, Achilles is overcome by anger after his beloved friend Patroclus is killed by Hector in the battle of Troy. Achilles refuses to eat or rest before returning to battle to avenge the death. "You talk of food? I have no taste for food—what I really crave is slaughter and blood and the choking groans of men!" Achilles proceeds to ruthlessly slaughter whoever crosses his path to get to Hector. Rage can flip off our "humanity switch."

We are not permitted to choose the frame of our destiny, but what we put into it is ours.

—DAG HAMMARSKJOLD

In the Nyakyusa tribe of Indonesia, burial ceremonies include a war dance. As an old tribesman explained, "We dance because there is war in our hearts (*ukukina*). A passion of grief and fear exasperates us (*ilyojo likutusila*)....Death is a fearful and grievous event that exasperates those men nearly concerned and makes them want to fight."

How can we safely surface and release fury? Some therapy methods include beating on mattresses and pillows, ripping apart phone books, or even visualizing the destruction of whoever we hold responsible for our loss or misery. By fantasizing releasing the anger, these methods seem to release emotion and allow the letting go process to be completed. A friend described to me the amazing peace she felt after imagining that she ripped the head off her abusive brother, saw him dead, and felt the raw emotion. It was scary, but seeing the healthier relationship she now has with her brother, I recognize that this strategy can be effective.

My favorite anger-release method comes from the Buddhist teacher Phillip Moffitt: see rage or misery as a waterfall that is washing over me. By welcoming this emotion, I stand underneath its torrent, allowing it to just *be*. By recognizing that rage is a natural and necessary companion on my journey, I allow it instead of fighting against an emotion that I find to be embarrassing. In this way, Moffitt explains, we receive what is coming just as it is. In the acceptance of the anger or the other emotions of grief, we are able to bear them, and they can pass through us. I allow myself "waterfall days" during which I am not to do anything with the anger, just *be* in it.

How can you let the rage of injustice out without hurting another? I appreciate Sarah Lavely's sassy business venture designed to safely express frustration. Lavely had a lifelong passion for throwing things when really angry. "During my divorce," she said, "I broke a lot of stuff on my driveway." The idea for the Smash Shack came to her. She woke up one day with the thought *I really want to go break some stuff.* "I wished there was someplace I could go and just do that, just go nuts," she said. "I was sure other people felt like that at times, and I thought I should open a shop where you could do that." At Sarah's Smash Shack in San Diego, you can don coveralls, protective glasses, and gloves, and throw all sorts of breakables against a wall. Wine glasses, plates, vases, and saucers are available to write the injustices on, and then you can shatter them in a private room.

> *In the end, it seems that power has less to do with pushing leverage points than it does with strategically, profoundly, madly letting go.*
>
> —DONELLA MEADOWS

Meet Your Other Half

In myths about the Underworld, there is almost always a formidable being waiting there to meet us. The goddess Inanna meets her sister, Ereškigal, who is ugly, mean, and in excruciating pain. Upon Inanna's arrival, Ereškigal doesn't thank her for her kindness but strikes her dead by looking at her with glowing, red eyes and leaves her to rot on a hook. Similarly, the Greek goddess Demeter has to bargain with the Underworld's unsavory ruler, Hades, to take her daughter home. Buddha is visited by the demon Mara multiple times as he travels through the dark realms of consciousness. These myths tell us that we must negotiate with some nasty and dangerous forces.

Who are we to meet when we tread through our own murky places? The biblical Job gives us a clue. When we meet Job, he is the presentable and respected community leader, the career man, the good father and husband. He's the kind of guy you'd want to advise your business or to invite over to dinner. Job says, "As I walked to the square of the city and took my seat of honor, young men held their breath; old men rose to their feet; rich men stopped speaking and put their fingers to their lips." After great tragedy sends Job into chaos, it is as though his alter ego or his messier version appears. Job then becomes a sick, angry, and socially unacceptable guy. He says things that make people uncomfortable. He is mean, blasphemous, and rude. He is smelly and covered in boils. He is like the raving homeless guy that we try our best to ignore when walking down a city street.

The myths advise that the less-than-pretty or unacceptable sides of ourselves arise during murky times. We meet our "inner victim" or our sad or rage-filled side. In the depths of tough times, we can be vain, petty, and downright mean. Like Ereškigal, we can be ugly in our pain and don't play well with others. We are messy and miserable, and we understand why Ereškigal wants to knock off that Little Miss Perfect, Queen of Heaven and Earth, Inanna. She pisses us off—all pretty and put together while we feel like crap and can't begin to figure out how to piece our broken lives back together.

In India, the city of Benares is considered the ultimate place to be cremated and thrown into the sacred Ganges River. The elderly and infirm come from all over India to die within its walls, believing that they will attain immediate liberation or salvation as a result. Loved ones send thousands of corpses to be burned in this most sacred of Hindu pilgrimages. Death is ever-present in Benares, and the Aghori ascetics congregate there during the festivals of Lolark Chhath and Guru-Purnima. These strange old men embody the Underworld on this earth. It is said that they live on cremation grounds, dress in rags, or walk naked with a necklace of bones around their necks. Their demeanor is described as brusque and foul mouthed, and they have been reported to eat the flesh of corpses and drink urine. As a unique sacred practice, they have sexual relations only with prostitutes who are menstruating.

The practices of the Aghori ascetic mirror that of the god Siva, Lord of the Cremation Ground and the Conqueror of Death. The ascetics are considered gurus with supernatural powers. By turning the profane into the sacred, the Aghori remove the duality between life and death, good and bad, polluted and pure. In so doing, anthropologist Jonathon Parry explains, the "Aghori aims to suspend time, to get off the round-about and to enter an eternal state of Samadhi in which death has no menace."

Psychologists would say that it is in the dark of tough times that we meet our inner Aghori ascetic, our ugly sister, or as Carl Jung named it, our "shadow"—the aspects of ourselves that we'd rather not admit to. Who wants to recognize that they can be sly, rude, or vengeful? Western psychology and the spiritual traditions all add that, in meeting and appreciating these less desirable traits, we have the opportunity to become healthier and more authentic. As Jungian psychologist Robert Johnson explains, "To own one's own shadow is to reach a holy place—an inner center—not attainable in any other way. To fail this is to fail one's own sainthood and to miss the purpose of life." In a less-obvious way, like the Aghori, our work becomes to marry the sacred with the profane, the acceptable with our unacceptable, and return from tough times more fully ourselves.

I once met a woman who had renamed herself Megan, pronounced *mee-gan*. I asked why she chose this name, as my sister's name is pronounced the same. Megan said that after some dark times recovering from abuse, she took on this name because she was "me again." She shared that in the deepest visits through the chaos, she found the most valuable parts of herself. "It was like finding jewels in a dark well."

> *As life becomes harder and more threatening, it also becomes richer, because the fewer expectations we have, the more the good things of life become unexpected gifts that we accept with gratitude.*
>
> —ETTY HILLESUM

By acknowledging less attractive aspects of ourselves, we have an opportunity to become more balanced and whole. It is said that the demon Mara made many visits to Buddha throughout his life. When the evil one arrived, Buddha pulled up two cushions, set out two cups, and invited Mara to tea. Mara lost any power over Buddha, and harmony was restored.

> *Whenever you fall, pick something up.*
>
> — OSWALD AVERY

Sometimes, alter egos grant us relief. "After our mother died," Leslie said, "my sisters and I went home for the memorial service. She died way too young, and we were all a mess. One night, my siblings and I went to the high-school football game and cheered like wild women. We whooped and hollered and laughed until we cried. I'm sure others thought that we were drunk or just found us to be obnoxious. Instead, we were crazy with grief. We didn't act at all like grieving children should, but we really needed that night, and no one in the community said a thing."

Summary

Major transitions can be terrifying. Fear constricts our movement and brain process, so we want to actively create inner calm and rest.

These techniques drawn from common mourning practices can help:

1. *Slow down.* Create blocks of "recovery time."
2. *Give yourself a year.* Don't push yourself to "be normal" too soon. Twelve months is the standard adjustment period across cultures.
3. *Welcome all your feelings.* Notice what emotions appear and permit them to be.
4. *Allow anger.* The safe acknowledgement and release of rage supports greater peace.
5. *Meet your other half.* Know that less-accepted characteristics have a role in recovering from loss.

These techniques, and those in the following chapter, nurture mental and emotional health in Winter by creating space to let go. Our work in the dark and inhospitable part of the journey is to clear the emotional turmoil—to allow difficult emotions to come up, to be recognized, and to flow through. This can be tough work and is not likely to be on our "fun list, but it's worth the trouble.

CHAPTER 5

Eat, Drink, Play, Laugh

Imagination was given to us to compensate for what we are not; a sense of humor was given to us to console us for what we are.

—MARK MCGINNIS

Tough times sap our reserves. When I described tough times as a journey in a workshop, a participant who had taken the trip added, "That journey can take a while, so you might want to bring along supplies and a tent."

When we are worn down by struggle and suffering, we need sustenance and refuge. Taking care of ourselves in the best of times is important; during the worst times, it is critical.

Often depicted in story as a journey through the Underworld, the middle of tough times is dark, lonely, and so unlike everyday existence

> *The wise see that there is action in the midst of inaction and inaction in the midst of action. Their consciousness is unified, and every act is done with complete awareness.*
>
> —BHAGAVAD GITA 4:16–17

under good circumstances. Down deep, we can lose touch and forget what once brought us joy. It's as though our minds are washed with a gray film and our emotions are flattened. There are dark alleys within which we can get lost for years. We need some light to help guide us home.

While an apple a day might keep you out of the doctor's office, adding levity and nurturing every twenty-four hours is a great rule of thumb when difficult times come your way. When reviewing Richard Dowden's book *Africa: Altered States, Ordinary Miracles*, author Pam Houston noted that by the mid-1990s, thirty-one of Africa's fifty-three countries had been ravaged by civil unrest or war, yet there is no word in most African languages for depression. Dowden said, "Africa lives with death and suffering and grief every day, but to be alive is to talk and laugh, eat and drink—and dance."

Each of us contains an internal bucket or an internal bank account. When it's filled, we are full of energy. This resource can be used to nurture someone, start new projects, or brighten another's day. It's our enthusiasm, our spark, the light that we bring to others or use to help ourselves. When we are well rested and refreshed, we have lots of nurturing *juju* to give to the world. When an opportunity comes our way and we

> *All this hurrying soon will be over. Only when we tarry do we touch the holy.*
>
> —RAINER MARIA RILKE

have a hefty internal account, we have the optimism and the reserves to grab it and go.

Activities that require energy draw down our internal account, and experiences that give us joy fill the bucket. Just like a checking account, energy is withdrawn when we are active and deposited when we replenish ourselves.

Tough times create a hole in the bottom of the internal bucket. Fear taxes our systems and wears us out. The emotions of grieving can be exhausting. Looking for answers and dealing with the fallout of major transitions requires a lot of work, and the bucket can easily be sucked dry. When we are adjusting to new circumstances, we dip often into our bucket just to make it through the day.

When there is nothing left in the bucket, there is nothing left to share. It's hard to be a helpful employee, wife, mother, or friend if I have nothing more to give. If I am really parched, I may even come after your bucket. At an extreme in this state, we can become like vampires, sucking the life out of victims. I think of the stressed stage parent or soccer mom who uses her children's success or joy to grab a "hit" of happiness.

As responsible parents, partners, and coworkers, it's critical that we feed our internal reservoirs when dealing with difficult circumstances. We have to recover emotionally, intellectually, and sometimes spiritually and physically during tough times to get the bucket brimming over once more.

Eat, Sleep, Walk

I'd love to find a creative way to approach this next tip, but it's boring, basic physical care. Gently take care of yourself each day. Eat well, sleep, and get exercise. These allow you to recover, and they speed your adjustment and give you the strength to soldier on. Daily care goes from important to fundamental when difficult times appear.

As a virtual member of your caring community, I am goading you from afar. Our caring community is usually tasked with nagging and making sure that you eat, sleep, and get outside during a major loss. We bring casseroles and urge the mourners to eat a little. We watch that those we love are getting rest. We might have to get them out of bed and into some fresh air. After sitting shiv'ah in the Jewish tradition, a family walk is prescribed. With gentle nudges, the community's role is to draw you back to the land of the living when the time is right with food, drink, sleep, and exercise.

Going through a rough stretch that is not as visible as a death, you may not be provided with a friend or grandmother to keep after your care. It is really important that you remember to eat something healthy three times a day. Get six to eight hours of sleep a night and go for a half-hour walk or the equivalent at least five days a week. Ask someone from your team to keep after you on this point.

In the Taoist tradition, tough times call for a *yin*, or gentle, approach. During great transitions, we are not advised to aggressively run ten miles, eat only organic food, or have our head on the pillow at exactly ten o'clock. Replenish yourself kindly each day. At every decision point, ask yourself, "What would be the nicest thing I could do for myself?" or "What would make me feel good when I'm done?" Choose an approach that nurtures but doesn't require extra energy. Gather, rest, and allow. This recovery strategy can help you to be ready for the *yang*, or dynamic, activities that lie ahead.

When we are miserable, sometimes self-care goes by the wayside. Down or even depressed, we may see no use in eating well or exercising. These activities connect us to the living world, and by eating, we symbolically say that we want to be part of it. Because we feel disillusioned with the place that causes us so much pain, we choose this way to disengage. "I'm not playing anymore," I say as I turn away from caring for my body. At its worst, the thought becomes, "I don't care if I live or die." When not eating well, resting, and moving our bodies, we cycle into a darker and darker place.

Find a way to make these basic activities daily habits. This will keep you moving forward to new possibility; it is a prescription for faster recovery. You want out of the pain? Eating, sleep, and exercise will help you move out of it more quickly.

Play Each Day

In ancient Greece, days of sporting events were put on to honor a fallen warrior. At wakes, we sing. Mourning in West Africa includes dancing. To remember lost friends, we tell funny stories about them and feel better. We cook elaborate meals and bring friends together. Adding play or playfulness to tragedy lightens our load.

Finding time to play or do something that brings us joy feels counterintuitive when we are struggling. We want to put our nose to the grindstone to dig ourselves out of our troubles or just go back to bed. A Puritan work ethic makes doing something we love seem wrong or out of place, especially if other people are suffering too. However, a dear friend, Carl, who lived with chronic congestive heart failure said, "Who wants to have fun when you're sick, right? It's probably the very best time to create some diversion for yourself."

> *When we play we are engaged in the purest expression of our humanity, the truest expression of our individuality.*
>
> —DR. STUART BROWN

Dr. Stuart Brown has studied the science of play for over twenty years and believes that remembering what play entails and incorporating it in our daily routine is "probably the most important factors in being a fulfilled human being. The ability to play is critical not only to being happy, but also to sustaining social relationships and being a creative, innovative person."

Brown defines play as follows:

- It's apparently purposeless. We do it for its own sake.
- It's something we choose to do.
- It's fun and makes us feel good.
- Within it we lose a sense of time and stop worrying if we look good or silly.
- It creates potential to improvise or ways to shift our perspective.
- We want to keep on doing it, and when it's over, we want to do it again.

Brown believes that play is a state of mind, not one particular activity. For some of us, the practices of creating art (painting, sculpture, pottery), story (writing, theater, poetry), or movement (dance, sport, martial arts) are playful. Perhaps designing or tending a garden or playing with children lifts your spirits. For many of us, solving puzzles and playing games calls us. Ask "What brings me joy?" or "What reminds me that no matter how bad the circumstances, this world is worth the effort?"

When dealing with frustration or despair, it can be hard to recall what brings us joy, let alone add another activity to our day. We have a hard time drawing from the regions of the brain that house emotions of gratitude and joy. When working with struggling clients, I often hear, "I don't know what brings me joy. All I do is work and clean the house, and neither is remotely fun."

One way to recover play is to remember how you spent a free day when you were between eight and ten years old. Harvard researcher Emily Hancock details in *The Girl Within* that these in-between years are a brief window where many are left to their own devices. We are old enough to be allowed to chart our own course through a summer day, yet too young to be expected to work or take on major responsibilities. As a preteen, we are given the time and the freedom to figure out what we found to be fun. Ask yourself what you would have done on "a perfect day for fun" when you were nine.

> *The personal life deeply lived always expands into truths beyond itself.*
>
> —ANAIS NIN

When I hit rough patches, I have to make play a "must do," like brushing my teeth. When I'm struggling, it seems impractical or inappropriate to have fun. I justify it by reminding myself that by shifting my perspective to enjoyment, I push myself to move from a fight-or-flight, crazy-making state into my higher, neocortal regions. Being happy, creative, and grateful revs up my brainstorming/complex processing capabilities.

Additionally, play seems to expand brain processing and better prepares us for the future. Noted play researcher

Jaak Panksepp has shown that actively playing selectively stimulates "brain-derived neurotrophic factor (which stimulates nerve growth) in the amygdala (where emotions get processed) and the dorsolateral prefrontal cortex (where executive decisions are processed)." Animal play expert Bob Fagen believes that play teaches young animals to make sound judgments. After over twenty years of in-depth play study of Alaskan bears, he states, "In a world continuously presenting unique challenges and ambiguity, play prepares [bears] for an evolving planet."

What might seem like frivolous activities may open us to new solutions. Playing around can lead us to prototypes and novel options. As Brown explains, "The first steam engine was a toy. So were the first airplanes. Darwin got curious about evolution through collecting samples from the seaside and garden where he played as a kid.... We want to do this stuff not because we think paper airplanes will lead to 747s. We do it because it's fun."

> *Indeed, thought which tries to avoid play is in fact playing false with itself. Play, it appears, is the very essence of thought.*
>
> —DAVID BOHM

Need some playful suggestions? Here are favorites offered by clients and friends:

- Bird watching
- Playing Monopoly
- Watch every dawn for a month

- Horseback riding
- Singing in the shower really, really loud
- Roller skating
- Dancing around the kitchen
- Photography
- Going to an art museum
- Creating collages with old magazines
- Swapping funniest childhood stories
- Watching the NCAA Final Four

If you are really down, playing isn't going to make you feel better initially. Divorce had one of my friends in Winter's depths for almost a year. Everything seemed flat or gray. She loved sunsets and watched them nightly because they had once brought her joy, but the usual "I'm so happy to be alive" feeling escaped her month after month. She credits the joyful things that she had made herself do in her ultimate recovery as they reminded her that there would be light at the end of the tunnel. When you don't feel immediate joy, keep returning to play each day.

Carl, my friend with the chronic health condition, reminded me not only of the importance of play but also to be kind to ourselves when we choose an activity. In his case, during his last bout of illness, he needed constant connection to an oxygen tank. He chose to find joy by quietly looking at family photos of summer days spent at a lakeside cabin. For him, this was perfect medicine. It was calming and brought him great joy while not taxing his scant reserves.

Give Yourself the Giggles

> *If I had no sense of humor, I should long ago have committed suicide.*
>
> —MAHATMA GANDHI

Let's imagine that your house floods and your spouse leaves you. Your children refuse to speak with you and a dog just bit your leg. What's a person to do? Global advice is to start laughing.

Really—in situations like those, you have to laugh. From the practices of Hopi and Zuni ritual clowning to Zen Buddhism and modern philosophical writings, around the world, we are taught to regard laughter and comedy as critical disciplines. When the going gets tough, find a way to crack yourself up.

The Nyakyusa of Malawi have "funeral friends" whose job it is to tease, insult, and disrupt the dead and the bereaved. In many cultures in Africa and elsewhere, those at the edges of kinship (cousins, age mates, or relatives through marriage) are called "joking partners." As anthropologist Nigel Barley explains, "Yet theirs is also a serious job." As Kierkegaard once said, "It is certainly unjust to the comical to regard it as the enemy of the religious."

> *One must have chaos in oneself to be about to give birth to a dancing star.*
>
> —FRIEDRICH NIETZSCHE

Death itself is joked with during Mexico's Day of the Dead. It's a day of inviting the dead back to the land of the living to be entertained. Men dress up as women to dance, and bakers create sweets in the likenesses of skulls and skeletons. We need to laugh, especially when we are miserable or struggling with loss. Laughter helps us to back up so that we can see our situation with greater objectivity. It cracks open fixed beliefs, because comedy is based on displaying the ludicrous in what we might believe to be beyond reproach. By allowing ourselves to see the humor in the worst, we detach and notice where we are too rigid and missing an opportunity to move forward.

Zen Buddhists believe that enlightenment is accompanied with laughter. Koans and paradoxical statements like "hold tightly with an open hand" are meant to frustrate and confuse, to get us to back up and view the situation from a new perspective. I'm suspicious that the phrases given to initiates to meditate on for years might be jokes in disguise. Take this koan from the twelfth-century Zen *Book of Equanimity:*

Venerable Genyo asked Joshu, "When there is not one thing, what then?

Joshu replied, "Throw it away."

Genyo said, "With not one thing, what is there to throw away?"

Joshu remarked, "Then carry it off."

It feels like there's a punch line in there somewhere.

Hopi and Zuni ritual clowns of the American Southwest urge their communities to laugh at what they might take too seriously and to remember the bigger picture. They openly jest about motherhood, mourning, and power, for example, ensuring that all recall we are on the same rocky path and no one escapes alive.

I had to read about ritual clowning before my husband Bruce's morning routine got any respect. As an estate planning and business lawyer, he spends his day talking about the very serious subjects of death and taxes, but somehow he is a happy, and funny, guy. As one friend said, "Only your husband could get me doubled over giggling about picking guardians for our kids in our will."

I'm figuring out one of Bruce's secrets of sanity. Each morning from our bed, I hear coffeemaker gurgles and chuckles in the kitchen as Bruce reviews the prior day's late-night monologues from his laptop. His favorite website

> *When a people can laugh at themselves and laugh at others and hold all aspects of life together without letting anyone drive them to extremes, then it seems to me that people can survive.*
>
> —VINE DELORIA JR.

is http://laughlines.blogs.nytimes.com. He purposely calls in the clowns every morning to orient himself for the day ahead.

Another morning humor ritual is emigrating from India. In the past ten years, Dr. Madan Kataria has helped more than three thousand laughter clubs to organize across that country. Kataria and his fellow members practice "laughter yoga" each day to improve their health and well-being.

I leave you with a mental image from a wise and funny friend, David Baum, who worked as a clown in the Ringling Brothers Circus to pay his way through college. After emergency open-heart surgery in his early forties, he found himself quickly pulled out of bed to walk the halls by a bossy nurse. Chest aching, shaky, and miserable, he realized his predicament. He explained, "There I was, exposing my backside in the flimsy hospital gown, pushing an IV down the hall, and looking like hell. My doctorate degree and respected consulting practice were distant memories as I felt and probably looked like a ninety-year-old instead of forty-two, yet to make it down the hall, I found myself humming the opening song to *Bonanza*. You know, the one where they come riding into town... Really, what else could I do?"

Feed yourself physically, intellectually, and creatively. A coaching client came to me, frustrated by a lack of progress in developing a fulfilling writing career. "Why can't I sit down and write three hours a day? What is wrong with me?" she asked. It took a few questions to discover that having recently moved, and as a co-owner in a family business and mother of a teenager and eleven-year-old twins, she was exhausted. She had no energy left to give, let alone to be creative.

To get her on the road to recovering from the demands of business, motherhood, and moving, she allowed herself to be as lazy as possible for a month. That meant exercising less and caring less about what she ate. It also meant finding ways to have fun. How kind and loving could she be to herself? I asked her to watch what made her feel good and do it, to fill her bucket. After a month, exciting ideas about a new book poured forth for her.

Summary

Tough times drain our internal reserves. Without resources, we lack energy to adjust to changing circumstances and look for solutions to our problems. There are three key ways to fill your internal bucket:

- Take good physical care of yourself.
    a. Eat well.
    b. Sleep six to eight hours each night.
    c. Move your body.

- Play. Make sure to do something fun, something that brings you joy, each day.
- Laugh. How can you bring levity to your situation?

What makes you feel good? Have you laughed today? What have you done that makes you truly happy?

In the world's myths, heroes are often put under a spell. They fall into a deep sleep, are turned into stone, or lose their memory. The depths of tough times create the same state. Eating well, playing, and laughing wake us up. They are the elixirs sent from the land where a child's smile warms the heart, where a sunset fills us with happiness. They remind us that it's worth getting up after being knocked down and urge us to seek the warmth and light that Spring can provide.

Spring

In the depth of winter, I finally learned that within me there lay an invincible summer.

—ALBERT CAMUS

Overview

Spring! We have reached a time of new beginnings, of light appearing at the end of a dark tunnel. Surrendering and taking time to recover in the second phase—Winter—sends us on a trajectory toward the new and possible. For example, the thought "this job is terrible and it needs to go" in Winter opens us to consider what might be better work. The willingness to look at our situations in new ways moves us forward. Spring—the third phase—brings hope and excitement, and it can be overwhelming. We are on our way back home, but we need to work actively to get there.

Doreen, who had recently retired, explained the third stage like this: "I was a nurse for many years, but it became time to let that go. My health and family were suffering. Now I have loads of time and am not sure what to do. There are so many possible volunteer opportunities. I could write. I could read, hike, or do nothing. It's kind of unnerving after knowing exactly who I was for thirty years. Right now, I'm just trying to stay open to find what is right."

How Are You Feeling? Excited, Overwhelmed, Pressed for Time

After the sadness and hopelessness of Winter, when we recognize that there can again be joy some day in the future, we transport ourselves into the third stage. It's a relief after the hard beginnings of tough times to recognize that we might someday feel happy again. After the travels thus far, we can feel raw or "broken open," as author and teacher Elizabeth Lesser calls it. Once we cracked open by our circumstances, light or hope finds new ways to seep in, and excitement appears.

With new possibilities, unexpected challenges also arise. If we have dealt with a traumatic event, depending on what occurred, the thought of returning to work, entering a relationship, or driving a car might feel overwhelming. If the fire was hot and I got burned, I might not be remotely interested in cooking ever again. I might ask, "How could I ever figure out a good choice when my last decision caused all that pain?"

How You Can Get Stuck

Those stuck in Spring may say,

- "Love hurts, so I'm going to go it alone."
- "People are selfish; it's not worth helping another."
- "Democracy is a crock, so why would I vote?"
- "I'll show up to the job, but why should I care?"

To create safety, we may try to insulate ourselves. If you lost a job that you loved, one survival option is to not care about where you work. We take the treasure that we've got left and act like dragons guarding it. We refuse to open our hearts and minds to what the world might offer. We build fortresses around our possessions and our hearts.

Cultural anthropologist Angeles Arrien describes this refusal as losing connection to the Four Rivers of Life. When we are connected to the rivers of Inspiration, Love, Surprise, and Challenge, according to many traditional societies, their healing waters can sustain us. However, when we are unwilling to open ourselves to inspiration, love, surprise, or challenge, we begin "walking the procession of the living dead." We stay in the loss and sadness, and refuse to reengage in everyday life.

It's as though our essential nature went on a walkabout into the depths of the Underworld and does not want to come back home. Think of those who do not regain their enthusiasm after a great loss. They are here physically, but in their eyes or voices, there is no spark. They are unwilling to be surprised, to risk in love, and to be challenged in new ways. The body is present, but the soul isn't.

How to Make It Through: Listen for New Options

My children grew up riding horses. They (and I) have all been bucked off more than once. Barn wisdom is that you always get back on the horse. Our young offspring protested, saying that they would never ride again. Some of my best parenting appeared when I refused to budge until they got back on the horse. When our eldest son, Cameron, was a teenaged wrangler, he had a runaway horse that eventually threw him and broke his arm. Barn wisdom had him back on the horse and riding to the ranch until the pain in his arm became too great. Once his arm was in a cast, he went back to work. Today he's an excellent rider and a fearless individual.

> *To be nobody-but-yourself—in a world which is doing its best, night and day, to make you everybody else—means to fight the hardest battle which any human being can fight; and never stop fighting.*
>
> —E. E. CUMMINGS

If in Autumn we get bucked off and during Winter we lie on the ground and recover, in Spring we need to get up off the ground. It's time to dust ourselves off and start brainstorming how to get back on the horse.

Hard as it may feel, no matter what bucked you off, to get out of this phase, you have to decide to be willing to try again. You don't have to ride yet; that's coming up next. In Spring, you get to practice waiting just long enough and not grab the first steed that comes along. If you can listen for opportunities and notice how you respond to each possibility, you'll have a better chance of finding the right one to transport you back to stability. If a new option fills you with energy yet feels simple and elegant, you are probably on the right track.

CHAPTER 6

Celebrate

What we witness we are changed by, when we are witnessed, we can never go back.

—ANGELES ARRIEN

When a workshop participant suggested a metaphoric tent and supplies for the "tough-times trip," she said, "I try to remember that it is a journey and one that we are supposed to finish. Pitch a tent, but be careful that you don't build a house."

> *You cannot prevent the birds of sorrow from flying over your head, but you can prevent them from building nests in your hair.*
>
> —CHINESE PROVERB

It can be seductive to stay in the middle of tough times. Can you think of a friend who remains a victim of her divorce decades after the event? Or a sibling who can't seem to figure out his next job after years of exploring possibilities? It is easy to get stuck in the thick of the tough-times journey.

Rituals and celebrations help us accept changes and adapt. In the West, we celebrate graduations, weddings, and funerals. We can also smooth our way through tough times by celebrating the little endings we encounter. When a job, marriage, or societal role is done, it is good to mark each completion using the five simple components of a good party. We create an effective closing for one phase of life so that a new one may begin.

Simple rituals or celebrations that honor an ending help to get us back on our feet. It may be a party when a coworker leaves a job or a dinner acknowledging the signing of divorce papers. We overtly mark the loss and at the same time create space for those in the transition to *be* in it. No more pretending; we acknowledge that what is done is truly done. Even if I have been denying a passage or am furious or depressed, a ritual publicly signals completion and pushes me to adjust.

Celebrating is often the last thing we want to do. We would rather ignore the passage, because remembering brings sadness or maybe embarrassment. Focusing on a failed business, a deceased parent, or a lost job can hurt. If I can pretend that these aren't true, I might be able to live in the past a while longer, but I am only postponing pain. As anthropologist Ronald L. Grimes explains, "In the long haul, however, people often regret their failure to contemplate a birth, celebrate a marriage, mark the arrival of maturity, or enter the throes of a death. . . . Unattended passages become spiritual sinkholes around which hungry ghosts, those greedy personifications of unfinished business, hover."

We struggle with comprehending that an experience or a relationship is complete. Human propensity to create stories and habits seems to play into this difficulty. For example, if I ask you about your family or your work, you will tell me a story. I'd tell you that I am a mother of three, married for twenty-six years to an attorney, and live in Bozeman. When I was younger, I would have led with "I am the oldest of four daughters, and I grew up in downtown Minneapolis." These facts may be true, but they color how I perceive myself. If I tell the story often enough, it becomes my reality, even though some of the details or roles have changed.

When I am coaching parents, I notice how sometimes the stories we tell about our children reflect a long-passed reality. We may treat our offspring as though they are young and need minute-by-minute concern. However, if they are teenagers or adults, they can be given personal responsibility and recognition that we are no longer the center of their universes.

Who wants to let go of good thing? In the parenting example, when our children are young, we have purpose. "I'm a busy, young mother" is rarely preferred to "I'm an older woman alone at home." When the toddler won't sleep, having an empty house sounds grand, but in general, losing the companionship and sense of purpose that children bring can be tough. We want to hold on to the good stories as long as we can, but ask adults whose parents still treat them like ten-year–olds how good it is. When it's time, it's time. There are windows when we need to consciously shift to a new story and way of conducting ourselves.

> *So tonight I'm gonna party like it's 1999!*
>
> —PRINCE

Celebrations like graduations and weddings push us to move on. When we overtly acknowledge an ending, we are more apt to face facts and adapt. I believe this is a leading reason why funerals and mourning rituals are the most highly celebrated and elaborate of all rites of passage around the globe. When a loved one has died, the act of publicly celebrating this ending with our community makes it harder to pretend otherwise.

In 1929, anthropologist Arnold Van Gennap published the seminal book *Rites of Passage*, in which he described the universal practice of marking major transitions within communities. Major transitions include birth, adulthood, marriage, initiation, demonstration (public acceptance of a skill), mastery, and death. If it is time to let one's childhood die and become an adult, the proper initiation must occur. Cross-culturally, letting go or mourning is considered an important rite of passage that must be completed so we can reenter the community in a new role.

When discussing the Dagara tradition in Burkina Faso, Sobonfu Somé explains that when there is great loss, separation rituals are needed. When someone dies, "you have to undo the union" of spouses or other family members. She says that, like when the umbilical cords of children are cut, the bond is not gone, but "their life support sources change in order for them to survive." In that culture, separation rituals sometimes involve symbolically cutting something like a vine or one's hair. They also include ceremonies of cleaning the house and giving away all the clothes and belongings of the deceased. After the mourning period, there is a welcoming ritual in which others of their gender shower the widow or widower with water. Women are welcomed back into their parent's' home and the husband's family home, and they are able to choose where they wish to reside.

Creating a celebration, however small, can be an excellent way to move us along, whatever the change. Actions that I have witnessed that supported another's adjustment include the following:

- Going-away parties when someone is moving, leaving a job, or going to college
- Walking through a family home with siblings and friends after it has been sold. In each room, memories of what occurred there are brought forward

- Giving away maternity clothes to another mother. While passing them along, the giver shows each item, explaining which ones were her favorites and sharing much-loved memories.
- Birthday fetes
- Bachelor parties
- Cleaning out old files, noticing what they held, and why they are no longer necessary
- Getting rid of clothes that are too big or will always be too small or are not age-appropriate

> *I celebrate myself, and sing myself, and what I assume you shall assume, for every atom belonging to me as good belongs to you.*
>
> —WALT WHITMAN

When I left IBM after twelve years, my sister wisely suggested that we go out to dinner with friends and family. At the dinner, she presented me with a cake on which she had written in frosting "IBM" with a red circle-and-slash symbol over it. She had also drawn stick figures of me engaged in my favorite activities to remind me what may await me. It had been a good tour of duty, and she knew that I was anxious about what lay ahead, but she recognized that I needed to move on.

By studying ritual, I have learned that there are five key components of a good ending celebration:

- Invite others to celebrate with you. It's hard to pretend that something hasn't changed when your community has acknowledged otherwise.
- Take time to consciously face the ending. In a funeral setting, this is the common practice of mourners viewing the body. The wake pushes us beyond pretending, and in that acknowledgment, we help the brain to adjust.
- Create a symbolic action. With divorce, this might be selling the wedding ring, giving it to your child, or taking it to a jeweler to be reset. At funerals, we close the casket, pass out cards containing a photo of the deceased, and throw dirt into the grave. In many cultures, burning or giving away objects marks endings.
- Acknowledge what you had. What did you get from the experience and will be sad to let go? By noticing what you are losing, you are better able to grieve it and move on.
- Change something about yourself. As we will explore more in the following chapter, in many cultures mourners cut their hair after a death or pierce or scar themselves at the end of childhood. What might help you remember that the ending has occurred and that you are standing in a new life?

Show Up

The graduation and wedding season begins each May; it's time to dust off the suit and pay for appropriate presents. At these sometimes expensive and awkward experiences, many people wonder why they have to appear. Looking at these and other rituals, my advice is to tie the double Windsor or throw on the high heels and go.

> *Act as if what you do makes a difference. It does.*
>
> —WILLIAM JAMES

Our community supports us by encouraging and attending celebrations that mark endings and new beginnings. It meets us where we are and acknowledges our transition. As attorney Deirdre Sullivan explains, a caring community member should show up when we are commemorating a major loss:

> I believe in always going to the funeral. My father taught me that.
>
> The first time he said it directly to me, I was 16 and trying to get out of going to calling hours for Miss Emerson, my old fifth grade math teacher. I did not want to go. My father was unequivocal. "Dee," he said, "you're going. Always go to the funeral. Do it for the family."

So my dad waited outside while I went in. It was worse than I thought it would be: I was the only kid there. When the condolence line deposited me in front of Miss Emerson's shell-shocked parents, I stammered out, "Sorry about all this," and stalked away. But, for that deeply weird expression of sympathy delivered 20 years ago, Miss Emerson's mother still remembers my name and always says hello with tearing eyes.

Though a celebration might focus on one family member, it also supports the transition of others within the group. Puberty, graduation, and marriage rituals signal change for both the child and the parents. Funerals publicly mark a shift both within the family and within the structure of a community.

We tend to hide from celebrations because they can cause stress. The ground shakes underneath, as we must recognize that we haven't practiced the next phase. Celebrations push you to recognize that regardless of whether you are a celebrant or a friend, you have aged; you may now have children who are old enough to marry, or you may be the last living member of your generation. These facts can elicit grief as you realize that your own life is passing.

I've come to think of my community as organized in concentric circles with me at the center. My inner circle of family and friends surrounds me and is surrounded by a middle circle of acquaintances, and the outer circle is comprised of others in my "tribe." Your tribe might be your town, country, the greater human race, or all living things, depending on your viewpoint.

Within each circle, there are further gradations. Within the inner realm, there are the friends you would call without hesitation at 3:00 a.m. versus the buddies you ring up until 9:00 p.m., first asking, "Is this a good time?" Among your family, there is the sibling with whom you shared a room and the distant cousin you met once. The former example of each pair would be placed in a closer circle than the latter.

In our culture, we usually invite portions of our inner circle to our ceremonies. However, not clearly knowing which subcircle everyone belongs to can create messiness. You can invite too many and appear to be trolling for graduation dollars or attention, or you can send a specific invitation and offend a family member. Although I believe ceremonies are important, I would be hard pressed to appear at every event to which I have been invited. Choosing who to invite and how to respond can create disequilibrium.

I suggest erring on the side of going to a celebration. Sincere support is always welcome. As one friend said, "There were two events about which I still question if I should have attended. The first was a gathering of friends around a woman who had suddenly lost her husband. We had recently become friends, and I wasn't sure she would want me there to comfort her. The second was a funeral of the mother of my daughter's friend. I didn't know the mother yet cared for the child. It still bothers me that I should have gone to both."

Summary

Mark the ending of a job, a relationship, or any major shift by having some sort of celebration. To effectively celebrate,

- Invite others.
- Include an activity that symbolizes that the ending.
- Consciously face the facts.
- Give thanks for what you had and acknowledge the good.

Ritual and celebration have long been used to foster adaptation. Whether a young man returning from war or the birth of a new baby, celebration pushes us to recognize our roles and where we stand as a community. We can use celebration and symbolic gestures as a tool to move us firmly from what was into taking advantage of the new that comes with Spring.

CHAPTER 7

Mark the End and a New Beginning

Art will remain the most astonishing activity of mankind born out of struggle between wisdom and madness, between dream and reality in our mind.

—MAGDALENA ABAKANOWICZ

In the myth "Gawain and the Green Knight" King Arthur's most trusted knight, Gawain, must go on an arduous adventure into northern Scotland in the depths of the winter, and he suffers great hardship. After he finally meets the Green Knight and passes one critical test while failing another, he is able to return to Camelot. This story isn't complete until Gawain shares everything, both successes and failures, with the other knights. To help him remember what he has learned and return to stability, he puts on a green armband, which the other knights also wear, in solidarity, the rest of their days. Your journey through tough times is not done until you demonstrate that you have changed.

Anthropologist Arnold Van Gennep describes the three phases in a rite of passage as *separation*, *transition*, and *incorporation*. During tough times, we are yanked out of the old way of being—separated from comfort and sometimes from those we loved or work we enjoyed. These are the wintery, dark times of transition. During initiation rites into leadership, priesthood, or other special roles within a community, transition is when the old identity is purposely destroyed. After an initiate is separated from his tribe, the elders strip him of habits and pride so that he will more readily adapt to his new role. Finally, at the end of difficult challenges, we are ready to return home and be reincorporated in our community.

In many cultures, a ritual washing or baptism of sorts symbolizes rebirth; those who have been in transition are welcomed home and incorporated back into the community. In some cultures, sharing a story facilitates incorporation, as was the case for Gawain. The other knights chose to wear the green armband, signaling their acceptance of the new and improved Gawain back into the group. Around the world, new names are also given as initiates into adulthood or a religious order are reincorporated into their communities.

How can the learning won through a tough initiatory process "stick" for the benefit of both you and your community? How can you give your experience a concrete form so that it is not forgotten? If you learned through tough times to slow down and enjoy your children, how will you remember this each day? If you know to be more compassionate with yourself and others, how can that become a habit? If life's fragility has become clear, what will bring this fact to you each morning? How can your journey now inform your life? How can you make the transition and incorporation process complete?

> *Music expresses that which cannot be put into words and that which cannot remain silent.*
>
> —VICTOR HUGO

How do you explain what you have learned in the depths of tough times, when the experiences and insights go beyond words? Psychoanalyst and author Thomas Moore provides some insight, "In your dark night you may learn a secret hidden from modern people: the truth of things can only be expressed aesthetically—in story, picture, film, dance, music. Only when ideas are poetic do they reach the depths and express the reality." As Ralph Waldo Emerson once said, the poet "stands one step nearer to things." Moore suggests trying to express what you have learned through artistic means using story, images, metaphors, and symbols.

John of the Cross used "the dark night of the soul" to describe the contemplative journey through spiritual tough times. He employed poetry to commemorate his trip through the depths. Some of his poems detail great suffering and loneliness:

> Where have you hidden
> Beloved, and left me moaning?
> You fled like the stag
> after wounding me;
> I went out calling you,
> but you were gone.

In the last verse of his final poem, he wrote,

> How gently and lovingly
> you wake in my heart,
> where in secret you dwell alone:
> and in your sweet breathing,
> filled with good and glory,
> how tenderly you swell my heart with love.

The authors of the book of Job employed story and metaphor to describe the journey they must have taken. Job poetically exclaims, "If ever my grief were measured or my sorrow put on a scale, it would outweigh the sands of the ocean: that is why I am desperate. For God has ringed me with terrors, and his arrows have pierced my heart." To help us understand how vast and intricately interconnected the universe is, God explains, "Do you tell the antelope to calve or ease her when she is in labor? Do you count the months of her fullness and know when her time has come?...Her little ones grow up; they leave and never return." To express his enlightenment, Job responds by saying, "I have spoken of the unspeakable and tried to grasp the infinite....I had heard of you with my ears; but now my eyes have seen you. Therefore I will be quiet, comforted that I am dust."

Employing Your Creativity

International consultant and artist Mary Corrigan knows that *creativity* and *art* can be seen as the C and A words within the corporate world. Corrigan's organizational development program, Creativity for the Rest of Us, "conspires to unleash the creativity we are holding in exile." She says, "Human beings are inherently creative. If you like gardening, you are an artist. Cooking is a creative art. There are loads of ways to express your innate wisdom and natural creativity. It's from this source that you can better run your company, foster creative environments where employees can innovate and develop exciting new products." Poet and professor Frank X Walker concurs: "I believe in a broad definition what of art is and who artists are: Barbers, cooks, auto detailers, janitors, and gardeners have as much right to claim artistry as designers, architects, painters and sculptors."

In different cultures, creativity is recommended as a tool to express learning and move forward. According to the Hopi people, "It is impossible to separate the activities of daily life, religious observation and artistic creation." In the Hindu texts the Upanishads, we are reminded, "Where there is creating, there is progress. Where there is no creating, there is no progress: Know the nature of creating." In the Islamic tradition, the Sufi poet Hafiz said,

> *The imagination is a great friend of possibility.*
>
> —JOHN O'DONOHUE

Art is, at last the knowledge of
Where we are standing—
Where we are standing
In this Wonderland

Educator and author Rev. Matthew Fox, who included art as a meditation as a core requirement in his institution's doctorate program, states, "As [the German mystic Meister] Eckhart put it, 'What is truthful cannot come from outside in; it must come from inside out and pass through an inner form.' All artists know this, and all persons need to learn it." Fox also says, "Clay doesn't lie when your hands work it, your body doesn't lie when it dances." Art is a form of truth-telling and grounding insight into reality.

> *I believe that what we often call survival skills is simply creativity at work.*
>
> —FRANK X WALKER

I asked Mary Corrigan what she recommended for nonartists to integrate the journey through tough times. Her suggestions draw on the seven areas of intelligence developed by educational expert Howard Gardner:

- Bodily-kinesthetic. Choreograph a dance, do yoga-like movements, create an improvisational skit in mime, or build a 3D model.
- Logical-mathematical. Create a "quilt" with images from magazines or your own drawings. Make a board game or "journey map" of what you don't want to forget. Write an outline and use imagery to illustrate it.
- Verbal-linguistic. Write a short story, fable, or one-act play of your experience. Write a poem or haiku. Cull the seeds of your experience into a few key words and make a mobile. Write and decorate an affirmation for yourself and post it where you can see it daily.
- Musical. Write a song or create a melody. Find a piece of instrumental music that captures the feeling of your experience and download it to your MP3 player. Make a "mix" tape, create a rap, or orchestrate a rhythm using body percussion.

- Visual-spatial. Paint, draw, doodle, cartoon, sculpt, build, or create a visual map, collage, poster, box (think treasure chest), or any object.
- Intrapersonal. Ask reflective questions: What is at the heart of this experience for me? Where was I surprised, touched, inspired, or challenged? Journal your answers. Declare an action that you will take to integrate your experience. Track your dreams and daydreams, and follow where they lead.
- Interpersonal. As you go through your day, look for all the ways the elements of your learning are all around you. Teach someone else what you've found.

Something to Wear

Concrete visual reminders can help us move closer to the end of our journey. A common grounding approach is to carry a symbol for the completed rite of passage, like Gawain's green armband. It might be wearing jewelry, like a wedding ring that demonstrates a consecrated marriage. One of my closest friends, Katherine, chooses to wear her mother's earrings every day since losing her to cancer. An acquaintance wears a ring that she bought to "marry herself" and thus commits to always treat herself with high regard.

In some cultures, tattoos, piercing, or scarring is used to denote the attainment of an initiation. Some of us naturally gather scars as a result of tough times, be it through an accident or surgery. As Dr. Rachel Naomi Remen explains in *My Grandfather's Blessings*, "Sometimes a wound is the place where we encounter life for the first time, where we come to know its power and its ways." Remen goes on to share the biblical story of Jacob, who wrestled an angel and wounded his leg. As the angel left, he touched Jacob on that spot, not to heal it but to remind him of the battle. Jacob carried that wound the rest of his life.

> *If you spend some time thinking about old age, death, and these other unfortunate things, your mind will be much more stable when these things happen.*
>
> —HIS HOLINESS THE DALAI LAMA

Cultures have also used clothing to indicate a rite of passage. Our grandfathers graduated to long pants at a certain age as they left childhood or might have been provided a special uniform to denote a role earned in a community. The colored belt of the martial artist is a centering reminder of what has been learned and the resulting responsibilities. The flowered skullcaps my friend wore while recovering from chemotherapy became her reminder of where she stood as a cancer survivor and to be kind to herself.

Changing the hair is another cultural symbol of letting go of the old and returning anew. In New Guinea,

Fiji, and India, mourners shave their heads. Within some of the First Nation people of North America and Australia, mourners or all community members cut their hair. Within other cultures, such as Greece or Bulgaria, beards and hair are not cut during the mourning period.

Once you have commemorated an event, you may wish to create a daily tradition to remind you of what you don't want to forget. Daily traditions are a standard multicultural approach to remembering and changing habits. It could be reciting a particular prayer, counting your blessings, or singing and repeating a commitment you have made. It could be putting on a ring or an article of clothing while remembering why it is worn. It might be looking at a scar on your nose that reminds you of life's fragility. With a daily practice, you remember your priorities and how you wish to conduct yourself during the day.

Summary

Humans are symbolically focused—that's why advertising is so darn effective. Create your own symbol to remind you to leave the past behind.

- Art, song, poetry, story, and dance are common cross-cultural strategies to create a lasting symbol of an experience and facilitate lasting change.

- Wearing a symbol can also be a consistent reminder of moving ahead.
- Creating a daily routine can symbolize what you don't want to forget and create new beneficial habits.

After we have found a way to commemorate our trip through creativity, a symbol, or a daily habit, we are ready to be incorporated into the everyday world. We are just about done, yet effort lies ahead. As we move back to the stability of Summer, we must show up and perform as our new, post-tough-times selves. We are called to have courage to reengage. The assistance we need to get us home is actually found in the support we are able to provide to others.

Summer

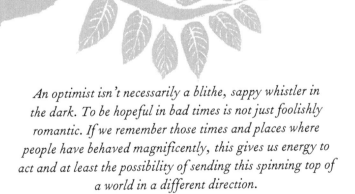

An optimist isn't necessarily a blithe, sappy whistler in the dark. To be hopeful in bad times is not just foolishly romantic. If we remember those times and places where people have behaved magnificently, this gives us energy to act and at least the possibility of sending this spinning top of a world in a different direction.

—HOWARD ZINN

Overview

We have survived the loss that Autumn brought. We have garnered strength in Winter to begin again in Spring. We can complete our tough-times journey if we are willing to tend the new garden of possibilities. In Summer, we must roll up our sleeves and get to work. Like my brave friend Jenny McCune, who after a spinal cord injury relearned how to walk and later to cross-country ski, you may also have to expose yourself to a good amount of failure. As Jenny says, "You have to get really comfortable with the risk of falling."

Summer's warmth and light has returned to our lives. We can now see a path home and have some ideas on how to get there, but we need to gather the courage to act. It's scary to try again or love again, but we are back on more solid footing, and so there is also often a sense of relief.

What Are You Feeling? Anxiety and Relief

This busy, action-packed stage brings anxiety along with it. We get nervous about the steps we need to take to get back on the proverbial horse. If you have decided to date again after a terrible breakup, you might have to gather the courage to make a call to schedule a dinner date. If you decided to enter the job market after a difficult divorce, you have to write that resume.

Remembering our past struggles can also create anxiety. During a workshop, I asked for this stage's attributes, and a kind, middle-aged professor said, "Nervousness! Even though now everything is good, I know that my life could fall apart again, and that someday it will fall apart again. You don't get to hang out in stability forever, you know."

However, surviving tough times mitigates this anxiousness. I am more confident. I fell into a pit and was able to reemerge. I might bear a few scars, but when I am in Summer, I'm back on my feet. This realization brings comfort. As Nietzsche reminds us, tough times didn't kill me, and I am thankfully stronger.

How We Get Stuck

To get out of the stage of Spring, we came up with ideas for the future. Using the example of addiction, say that I have decided to take good care of myself, go to AA, and give up alcohol. To make it back into the world, I need to act. I need to go to the meetings, choose new friends, and abstain. If I refuse to change, I stay stuck in tough times.

Circumstances throw us into difficulty. Financial mismanagement is another example. After suffering the misery of losing your house or perhaps all your savings, you may realize that you need to declare bankruptcy and no longer use credit cards. Yet, as long as you refuse to get your financial house in order, you won't find a stable solution. Tough times go away only in this case when you change your habits.

If we don't act on our plans, we'll make others miserable and might try to make those around us shift instead. We see this in an alcoholic's threats toward his family or in making a spouse or parent take responsibility for financial mismanagement. To find stability, we need to gather the courage and responsibility to change and find ways to help others along the way.

How to Make It Through: Try Something New—Act!

Kitchen-table wisdom is rife with sayings for this stage's guiding principle: "To win the lottery, you've got to buy a ticket," "Just do it," and "Winners don't quit, and quitters never win." Unlike previous stages, here we are called to committed action. We are invited to partake in life, and thus we must now participate.

In the Sumerian myth, the goddess Inanna barely escapes from the Underworld's depths. She is plagued by demons as she returns to earth. The demons remind Inanna that once you have visited the Underworld, you can leave only if you have someone to take your place.

This is a global common truth; to return home, you must give something back. Myth after myth explains that the tow of the Underworld is strong, that to return home requires committing fully to returning to the world. We must now act and give to others.

CHAPTER 8

Give Back to Come Back

For it is in giving we receive.

—SAINT FRANCIS OF ASSISI

Jerry White built his organization Survivor Corps around this principle: if you want to recover fully after tough times, it's critical that you give to others. Although being selfless sounds saintly, it is one of the more self-serving activities that we can perform. During difficult challenges, there is a time when we travel through the dark and can get lost in the depths. After this experience, volunteering our time or resources in some manner pulls us back into the world and exposes us once again

> *You can make more friends in two months by becoming interested in other people than you can in two years by trying to get other people interested in you.*
>
> —DALE CARNEGIE

to its joys and possibilities. By helping others, we help ourselves the most.

Generosity makes us reach out and reconnect. As a lovely Moroccan colleague noted, we are not alone in our pain. She explained,

> I lost two babies consecutively. The first was a stillbirth in the thirty-eighth week of pregnancy, and the second died on the second day after giving birth. It was so hard for me to go back to life. Two of my friends gave birth at the same time, and I still see their kids growing in front of me. For a time, I hated seeing babies around. I wanted to live in a place where there were no babies. I had to pretend that I was okay and people believed it.

> *They who give have all things; they who withhold have nothing.*
>
> —HINDU PROVERB

> Then, my aunt, who is three years younger than me, gave birth to her third child. The baby had a number of abnormalities and died after three weeks. I was the only person whose support was meaningful to my aunt.

> She told me many times that she drew strength from me and that she had no reason to feel down when she had me in mind. That was a great source of healing to me as well. I felt this [tragedy] did

> not happen only to *me*. I know it is cruel to think like this, but this is how I really got over it. I had been through a lot of strange feelings that I felt ashamed to share, but when I heard my aunt saying the same thing, I stopped blaming myself and knew they were so natural.
>
> Her loss was a mirror I could see my negative feelings in. Through her experience, I tolerated my annoyance at seeing babies. She had the same feelings, and she communicated them to me because she knew I would understand better than anybody else. Without knowing it, she was as great to me as she thought I was to her.

Generosity seems to help us stick around longer. A survey of 6,360 retirees revealed that after four years after the loss of their career, those participating in altruistic volunteer activities had a 14 percent lower death rate than those who chose not to volunteer. The community we serve helps by drawing us back to the surface from the Underworld.

> *Many persons have a wrong idea of what constitutes true happiness. It is not attained through self-gratification but through fidelity to a worthy purpose.*
>
> —HELEN KELLER

Sharing *or* sacrifice is also a common spiritual practice to create balance after societal disruption. Mortuary rituals include giving food, belongings, or money to the gods or larger community after a death. In the Pacific Northwest, the Tlingit community provides memorial potlatches, or parties, lasting four days during which the mourners shower guests from other communities with feasts, song, and gifts. Our modern-day gifts to memorial funds or providing flowers and casseroles can be enduring reminders of our ancestors' giving.

Sharing what we've learned is another powerful way to give back. Psychologist Victor Frankl used his experiences in concentration camps during World War II to support others when they were suffering. He made meaning and friendship out of a terrible experience. In the same vein, the cofounder of Alcoholics Anonymous, Bill Wilson, once wrote, "While I lay in the hospital the thought came that there were thousands of hopeless alcoholics who might be glad to have what had been so freely given me. Perhaps I could help some of them. They in turn might work with others."

Jerry White, who lost his leg to a landmine, described a comfortable post-trauma life that includes four healthy children and a beautiful wife. But it wasn't until a young girl in Cambodia with one leg and crutches said to him, "You are one of us," that he fully recovered from the trauma. When he accepted that he was part of a global community injured by landmines, Jerry began looking for a way to give back what he had learned. Cofounding the Landmine Survivors Network and Survivor Corps, he worked tirelessly to ban landmines worldwide and to help victims become survivors. Meanwhile, participants have also been expected to become volunteers and guide the newly injured. Jerry knows that what appears selfless is a foundational requirement for recovery.

When I teach this tip in workshops and ask for comments, I feel like I get to open secret safe-deposit boxes and admire someone's best jewelry. I hear fantastic, shimmering stories from the participants about how they have given back. One young teacher was one of the middle children of six kids. When their beloved mother died, the family went into a deep depression. To come back, the children created a tradition that on their mom's birthday each year, they would all do random acts of kindness. They paid for another family's dinner or the toll of a car behind them. With each act, they left notes saying that their gift was in honor of their mother.

> *One of the deep secrets of life is that all that is really worth the doing is what we do for others.*
>
> —LEWIS CARROLL

This story reminds me of the Chinese and Mexican cultural rituals where veneration of the ancestors is an obligatory annual event. On November 2, or All Soul's Day, Mexican family members

> *The nectar of life is sweet only when shared with others.*
>
> —ADAM MICKIEWICZ

visit gravesites with a picnic for the inhabitants. They build altars and offer drink, candles, flowers, and food. One April, when visiting a friend of Chinese origin in Thailand, I witnessed family members returning home from around the country to honor the dead. We visited a small monument housing the bones of multiple ancestors and offered food to them. After a time, the living visitors consumed the food. I was told that if the eldest son is moving to a new home, it is his job to carry the bones with him and build a new monument if needed.

Choosing to Come Back

Through my research, I didn't find obligatory tasks for those who have weathered difficult circumstances. I expected to find clear roles for widows to help newly bereaved women, for example, but found nothing clearly stated. I wondered if I had approached the question incorrectly. Perhaps "giving back" isn't a required cultural practice because helping others has to be a very personal choice.

> *When I dig another out of trouble, the hole from which I lift him is the place where I bury my own.*
>
> —CHINESE PROVERB

Showing up in your community after tragedy is an individual test of courage and optimism. A few years ago, Jerry White and I were talking about how perplexing it is that some people recover from terrible circumstances against all odds, while others who have all sorts of resources never get back up. We couldn't point to one factor other than a firm personal decision to get up and get involved in the community. It seems like a foundational spot where we all have free will. I can't make you get back on your feet again; you have to choose to do so.

Tibetan Buddhism offers an interesting perspective on this choice. Buddhists believe that the soul comes into being and then is reincarnated potentially multiple times. During each lifetime, we are born, we learn, and we physically die. In this process of death and rebirth, we always have options. If we need to learn more, we can choose into which body or family we want to be born the next time. When we have reached a high level of wisdom, we can choose not to be reborn and instead head into nirvana, or we can elect to return to earth to help others.

Tibetan Buddhists call the place between death and rebirth where these choices are made the *bardö* state (*bar*, in between; *dö*, island or mark). In tough times, the bardö state would be the Winter or "messy middle" period after loss and before recovery. "In-Between Island" living isn't easy. Bardö states are described as potentially terrifying, because there we face what most scares us. Inner demons appear as visions or nightmares. Similarly, on life's in-between islands, or during the bardö of existence, we come face to face with our greatest fears. Thoughts like,

"I'll never find another job and will be out on the street," "My husband will leave me," or "I will never heal and will die" creep into our heads. We feel pain while we mourn our losses. We worry that we will be broke, maimed, or abandoned.

If we don't understand how reincarnation works, according to Buddhism, we aren't aware that we have choices in this in-between state. Depending on our knowledge, we may fearfully jump into the first body available and can land ourselves in a situation worse than before. However, if I understand the death/rebirth process and I can face my fears, I can select a better future.

Similarly, if I don't understand that in every difficult circumstance there is an opportunity to reincarnate into a better me, I might jump at the first solution I can find to avoid pain. I might choose a life where I drink heavily to run away from my fears. I might quickly marry so that I'm not alone but have an abusive spouse. Fear of suffering and ignorance of how the process works make for bad decisions.

According to Buddhism, if we base our decision on how we might help others, we learn to be unafraid of death/rebirth and can better play the game

As I look more deeply, I can see that in a former life I was a cloud. And I was a rock. This is not poetry; it is science. It is not a question of belief in reincarnation. This is the history of life on earth.

—THICH NHAT HANH

of life. It sounds flowery and sweet, but it is practical when you see it applied.

In 1927, Buckminster Fuller found himself contemplating suicide on the banks of Lake Michigan after losing his daughter to illness and his business. In his lowest moment, he made a choice to stay and embark on "an experiment, to find what a single individual [could] contribute to changing the world and benefiting all humanity." In his biography, he wrote of the deep joy he felt throughout the rest of his life as he developed inventions like the geodesic dome, sustainability strategies, and a compact, high-mileage car. In looking for solutions to serve the greater good, he was undaunted by failure and tragedy.

I was lucky enough to interview Nadwa Sarandah and Robi Damelin when writing *Worst Enemy, Best Teache*r. Each had faced horrid tragedies. Robi's Israeli son was killed by a Palestinian sniper while in required military service, and Nadwa's Palestinian sister was knifed to death on the West Bank while walking down a street. Both had been knocked down, but through The Parent's Circle, an organization committed to create peace in their region by refusing to seek revenge, they found a way to recover. By focusing on helping their community, they found both purpose and a degree of peace. Robi said, "I can speak in front of sixty thousand people without fear."

Many spiritual traditions call for an overarching commitment to selfless service as a way to overcome death. In the Hindu tradition, we learn in the Bhagavad-Gita that if we wish to connect to that which is eternal (Atman) and move beyond the cycle of death and rebirth, we are to dedicate our actions to the Divine and not be attached to an outcome for personal gain. This tenet is found in Judaism, Christianity, and Islam and is illustrated in the story of Abraham, who was willing to sacrifice Isaac.

By working to be of greater service and surrendering the need for a particular outcome, we become enlightened. Shifting our focus from personal pain to how we can be of use, we relieve our suffering. A willingness to let go of what we once held dear and to give to others allows us to live more richly.

Work as Love Made Visible: Playing While Giving

"Pleasure in the job puts perfection in the work," Aristotle wrote. We give best when joy is combined with purpose. I feel most fulfilled when I am both having fun and being useful to others. I think of Viktor Frankl, as he developed his logotherapy approach, or Buckminster Fuller's inventions. Their passion for the subject was clear, and that their work has been so helpful to others surely made it even more fulfilling.

Play expert Dr. Stuart Brown interviewed Nobel laureate Roger Guillemin and polio researcher Jonas Salk and discovered that they were simply playing every day in their laboratories. Brown described Guillemin's medical research of neurohormones as "joy as pure as that of a kid showing off a beautiful shell picked up at the seashore." Their discoveries have saved countless lives and alleviated suffering. Financial guru Warren Buffett describes this spirit of combining purpose with joy as "tap dancing to work."

> *All these understand the meaning of service and will be cleansed of their impurities.*
>
> —BHAGAVAD GITA 4: 30

What can you do that would be fun and also support others? In *Compassion in Action: Setting Out on The Path of Service*, Mirabai Bush advises the following:

- Be brave.
- Start small.
- Use what you've got.
- Do something you enjoy.
- Don't overcommit.

What small, fun thing can you do this week to help? While reserving your resources as you continue to recover, how can you give? Here are some ideas:

- Call or send flowers to someone you know is struggling.
- Give a few hours to a local food bank.

- Create a care package for a child at school or away in the military.
- Sit with someone who is ill or failing. Nursing homes appreciate those who visit or read to shut-ins.
- Listen to new readers at the elementary school.
- Walk dogs at an animal shelter.

Mirroring Bush's advice, author Dr. Rachel Naomi Remen says, "The thirty-seven years that I have been a physician have shown me that any of the stuff of our lives—our joys, our failures, our loves, our losses, even our sickness—can become the stuff of service. I have seen people use anything to bless life." We can use just what we've got.

Getting back to the surface after a visit to the Underworld can be tough. Kris, a workshop participant, described it is as though the depths keep trying to pull you back, like the demons of Inanna's story. The dark is seductive, like when you are trying to wake up from a nap and get pulled back into sleep. Kris said that she sees helping others as a shining sword that she uses to brush off the demons and light her way back.

> *Look for what has heart and meaning.*
>
> —ANGELES ARRIEN

Summary

Doing something kind for another will help you to recover from difficulties. Focusing on helping others enhances your chances for longevity and happiness.

- Practice selfish selflessness. What is good both for you and for another?
- Look for ways to provide what you've learned from your difficult circumstances.
- Choose simple and enjoyable ways to give. Don't overdo!

Isabel Allende cared for her twenty-eight-year-old daughter, Paula, who spent a year in a coma until her death. She wrote, "Give, give, give—what is the point of having experience, knowledge, or talent if I don't give it away? Of having stories if I don't tell them to others? Of having wealth if I don't share it? I don't intend to be cremated with any of it! It is in giving that I connect with others, with the world and with the divine. It is in giving that I feel the spirit of my daughter inside me, like a soft presence."

CONCLUSION

Our basic convictions must be tested and transmuted in the crucible of experience—and sometimes the more bitter the experience, the more valid the purified belief.

—MARGARET SANGER

A young Alaskan woman, Mary Cook, lost her fiancé when he fell off a roof to his death. At first she could hardly exist. While life continued on, "as though the bottom hadn't fallen out of my world," Cook was unable to do much of anything. Friends had to cook and clean for her that winter. She was miserable and embarrassed at her lack of energy, but an elderly neighbor consoled her by saying, "You are not doing nothing. Being fully open to your grief may be the hardest work you will ever do."

In an essay she wrote for National Public Radio, Cook concluded after the loss of her fiancé, "I am not the person I once was, but in many ways I have changed for the better. The fabric of my life is now woven with gratitude and humility. I have been surprised to learn that there is incredible freedom that comes from facing one's worst fear and walking away whole."

I asked one of my mentors, Jo Norris, how she remains so vibrant, healthy, and fully engaged at eighty-three. At an early age, her father and mother passed away. Her younger brother died of a heart attack in his early forties. Eight years ago, she lost her husband of forty years and, recently, her beloved sister. There have been other tragic disappointments along Jo's path, but I can talk with her about anything—sex, drugs, death, or child rearing. She travels all over the world and is always up for a wild, new experience. Despite all the loss, she also really loves me.

Jo's answer was, "I don't know really why I am in such good shape, but I have noticed that I have had to learn to love in different ways."

Plato believed that love is the pursuit of the whole. Jo's words reminded me of how I loved my husband in our early years versus how I now feel after the tests of parenting, mortgages, and aging. Time uncovered the awkward, the ugly, and the extraordinary within us both. When I say I love him now, it's a richer definition of that word, which has somehow become large enough that I wish for his happiness even if it means he isn't at my side. I'm definitely loving in a different way than I did at twenty-two and, I hope, more wholly. I won love's expansion through tough times, which seems to be the only way I garner such prizes.

Tom, a former high-school teacher, shared this story with me:

> As a science teacher in a small Catholic school, I was periodically asked to sit in other classes as a substitute. One day, I happened to be asked to cover a world religions class and introduce an elderly rabbi whose words I will never forget. The rabbi had interviewed those couples in his temple that had been married for more than forty years to uncover the secret of marital success. He told a group of high-school students that 'passion' was their common attribute. The students sniggered, but the rabbi knowingly smiled and said, 'This is not the kind of passion you are thinking of. You must have passion in a relationship. You must be able to hold another's passion and that includes their pain. It is com-passion. If you can suffer with another and witness all feelings, now, that makes for a long relationship. Suffer together, it bonds you forever.'

Teacher Kathleen McDonald says, "We confuse attachment with love. Attachment is concerned with my needs, my happiness, while love is an unselfish attitude, concerned with the needs and happiness of others.... A relationship free of unrealistic grasping is free of disappointment, conflict, jealousy, and other problems, and is fertile ground for the growth of love and wisdom."

My love affair with Life or the Universe has also evolved. I have had to learn to love in different ways, as Jo suggested. I first loved Life because she dished out a lot of good stuff: a loving family, good friends, and interesting work. Later, as Life and I logged time together, she has both let me down and thoroughly amazed me. When I now say I love Life, it is with full knowledge that she provides not only pink-orange-purple sunsets and how-can-you-be-so-extraordinary strawberries but also rip-you-apart heartbreak and cut-you-into-pieces illness. I love her differently than I did as a child. She tested and strengthened my devotion. In conflict terms, we have fought well. Perhaps I love Life more as we have suffered together, as the wise rabbi suggested.

A spiritual director, Kate, called me to share that her only son had eloped and she was now seeing him much less. The mother and son had always been close, so his absence caused her pain. At a recent open house for the couple, Kate was asked by her son to give the new couple a blessing. She said, "As I spoke, I watched him gazing at his new bride and at me with such love and joy. I realize that his new spouse's family allegiances may mean we might rarely see our son, but this is right. I want him to be happy. To really say I love you as a mother, it now has come to include knowing that true love may involve loneliness and loss."

We adore our young offspring—their infectious smiles combined with their complete dependence give our existence both deep joy and a profound sense of meaning, but they grow up and may need to move away. Favorite grandparents need to pass on. Someday I will too. I am happiest when I am running, hiking, or dancing around my kitchen, yet someday those particular options won't be available. Change is inevitable.

Thankfully, the world's cultural traditions offer us tools to make it through each transition of losing what we value and find a new way to love. If we can

1. see our struggles as a four-phased adventure,
2. surround ourselves with a supportive team,
3. hold a positive attitude,
4. slow down, allow our feelings, and give ourselves time to recover,
5. carry good food, laughter, and play in our "backpacks,"
6. celebrate what has ended,
7. remind ourselves from where we've come,
8. and look for ways to help,

we can ease our journey.

When Jo said, "I don't know," she mirrored the cross-cultural wisdom of approaching every situation with an open attitude. Martial artists call meeting every challenge with *shoshin* ("I don't know") or "fostering a beginner's mind." Around the world, it is believed that only through not knowing can we improve. If we don't have it all figured out, we are open to opportunities to find joy and purpose.

Jo reminds me of another grandmother. Sue was deeply admired professionally and personally by her long-term friends within a group I facilitated a few years ago. As we talked about surviving tough times, her friends urged her, "Tell Deidre 'the one assumption!'" She smiled, threw up her hands with a giggle, and said, "The one assumption I always try to make is that I really don't know anything." As I made her acquaintance, it was clear that she knew a whole lot more than I did, and in that lay the poetry.

> *In the beginner's mind there are many possibilities, in the expert's mind there are few.*
>
> —SHUNRYU SUZUKI

Jo didn't advise, "Don't get attached." She didn't suggest I should love less so that it wouldn't hurt so much when change occurs. After eighty-plus years of experience, she gave no promises that tough times would ever be easy or avertable. Her advice urges us to continue to pursue loving, struggling, and adapting. I believe that not only Jo, but the world's cultural traditions urge us to use tough times to "look for the whole" of our children, loved ones, and Life in all her vagaries—to love it all, as Plato said. The world's cultural wisdom and the wise ones nudge me to keep getting back up, so that I can keep giving along the way. I *think* that is the overarching global wisdom informing this book, but I will never really ever *know*, will I?

TOUGH-TIMES CLASSICS

Success is not measured by what you accomplish, but by the opposition you have encountered, and the courage with which you have maintained the struggle against overwhelming odds.

—ORISON SWETT MARDEN

If you want a perspective shift that "it could always be worse" and ancient guidance from the tradition of storytelling, I refer you to the myths that I deem Tough-Times Classics. Some of the world's most popular and scariest stories are found in the "take you down so far that you scream at the heavens or find yourself in the Underworld" genre. Most of the Greek myths fit this description, as does the biblical book of Job. As a favorite example, I have next included the Sumerian myth of the goddess Inanna.

In addition to providing tips for dealing with tough times, these tales remind me that no one is exempt. If one of the most just and kind men of the Bible or even a goddess can't escape from battle, why should I? We are not bad people because we have been caught by a bad set of waves, let alone crushed. We are following a universal journey through wild and sometimes dark places. None of these stories contends that it will be easy or even that you will emerge again, but they demonstrate that it is possible.

QUEEN INANNA'S DESCENT INTO THE UNDERWORLD

This is a Sumerian tale from the beginnings of Egypt.

Inanna, the Queen of Heaven and Earth, decided to visit her sister, Ereškigal, in the Underworld. Had she heard that Ereškigal was sick, or was it her hope to be not only the Queen of Heaven and Earth but also of the Underworld? We aren't sure, but Inanna dressed in her best. Displaying her power, she wore a turban, a wig, a lapis necklace, beads, a *pala* dress (a garment of royalty), mascara, a chest plate, and a golden ring. She carried a lapis measuring rod. Off she set to see her sister, who was stuck alone in the depths.

At the first gate of the Underworld, the gatekeeper would let Inanna pass only if she gave up the measuring rod. "Why?" asked Inanna.

The gatekeeper replied, "It is just the ways of the Underworld."

To go through the next gate, she must give up her turban. She again asked why and was told, "It is just the ways of the Underworld." At the next gate, she had to give up her robes.

After passing through the seven gates, she had relinquished all her belongings so that when she arrived in front of Ereškigal, she was naked. Inanna made her sister rise from her throne, and down she sat.

Ereškigal was livid. She called seven judges, called The Anna, who rendered a decision against Inanna: death. They spoke with anger of Inanna's crimes. Through their words and looks, Ereškigal and The Anna turned Inanna into a corpse that was hung on a hook.

Before she had left, Inanna had instructed her servant Ninshibur to stand at the first gate and wait for her. She had implored Ninshibur to go to the gods Enlil, Nanna, and Enki to rescue her if after three days and nights she hadn't returned. So after three days passed, Ninshibur went to Enlil's temple, making sacrifices and banging drums. The loyal servant's pleas for help went unheeded as Enlil responded that Inanna had brought this on herself. Next, she went to Nanna and met the same reply.

Finally at Enki's temple, Ninshibur's cries were heard. Enki agreed to help Inanna, as he was troubled by her predicament. Using the dirt from under his fingernails, Enki created two sexless, flylike figures, neither male nor female, named Gala-tura and Kur-jara. Enki instructed them to calm and appease Ereškigal. If they were asked what they wanted in return, they were to request Inanna's corpse and sprinkle it with nectar and water of life, which Enki gave these Gala-tura and Kur-jara for their journey.

Gala-tura and Kur-jara flew undetected into the Underworld. They found Ereškigal in great pain, howling like a woman in childbirth. The Queen of the Underworld lived alone and was not allowed to visit any of the living gods. None were to visit her, because they would not be allowed to return home. When she moaned, "Oh, my head," Gala-tura and Kur-jara responded with compassion, "Oh, your head." When she ached and cried out, "Oh, my heart," they listened and responded, "Oh, your heart." Calmed and relieved of her misery, Ereškigal offered Gala-tura and Kur-jara fields of grain, great rivers, or whatever their hearts desired. They asked for only the green meat that was once Inanna, still hanging on a hook.

Gala-tura and Kur-jara revived Inanna with the nectar and water of life, and headed back to the land of the living. However, Ereškigal's demons hung onto Inanna, saying she would not be free to return home until she found someone to take her place in the Underworld.

They first came upon Ninshibur, waiting at the first gate, dressed in sackcloth, mourning her mistress. The demons cheeped, "Let us take her." Inanna knew that it was only because of Ninshibur that she was alive, and she said, "No, you may not take her." They next saw her children, who were also in mourning, and she again refused the demons.

When they saw Dumuzi, Inanna's husband, Inanna was livid to see that he was sitting in regal clothing and enjoying himself as though she had never left. Giving him the "look of death" that Ereškigal had given her, Inanna said, "Take him!"

NOTES

Introduction

To exist is to change, to change...Henri Bergson, *Creative Evolution* (New York: Holt, 1911), 7.

Suffering is the sandpaper...Ram Dass, *One-Liners: A Mini-Manual for a Spiritual Life* (New York: Random House, 2002), 79, 85.

I awoke each day...Jenni Lowe-Anker, *Forget Me Not: A Memoir* (Seattle: Mountaineers, 2009), 2.

Let me not pray to be sheltered...Rabindranath Tagore, *The Heart of God: Prayers of Rabindranath Tagore*, ed. Herbert F. Vetter (New York: Tuttle, 1997), 39.

It was a terrible blow to my faith...Helen Keller, "Light of a Brighter Day," in *This I Believe: The Personal Philosophies of Remarkable Men and Women*, eds. Jay Allison and Dan Gediman (New York: Holt, 2006), 139, 141.

It doesn't really matter what causes ...Pema Chödrön, *When Things Fall Apart: Heart Advice for Difficult Times* (Boston: Shambhala, 1997), 17.

Chapter 1: To Everything There Is a Season

Every problem has in it the seeds ...Norman Vincent Peale, *Enthusiasm Makes the Difference* (New York: Fireside, 2003), 127.

In my own experience, the period...His Holiness the Dalai Lama, *Kindness, Clarity, and Insight* (Ithaca: Snow Lion, 2006), 19. This quote continues with the question, "What gives you this chance? Your enemy..."

Brain research shows...Dan Baker, *What Happy People Know: How the New Science of Happiness Can Change Your Life for the Better* (New York: Rodale, 2003), 80, and John J. Ratey, *A User's Guide to the Brain: Perception, Attention and the Four Theatres of the Brain* (New York: Vintage, 2001), 171–72.

Autumn

Travelers, there is no path...Antonio Machado, "*Proverbios y cantares* XXIX" [Proverbs and Songs 29], *Campos de Castilla* (1912); trans. Betty Jean Craige, in *Selected Poems of Antonio Machado* (Louisiana State University Press, 1979). In Spanish, the poem states, "*caminante, no hay camino, se hace camino al andar.*"

Many societies acknowledge...Maria Cátedra, "Kinds of Death and the House," Jonathon Parry, "Sacrificial Death and the

Necrophagous Ascetic," and Robert Herz, "A Contribution to the Study of the Collective Representation of Death," in *Death, Mourning and Burial: A Cross-Cultural Reader*, ed. C. G. M. Robben (Oxford: Blackwell, 2004), 89, 199, 268.

Think of yourself as a general...Deidre Combs, *The Way of Conflict: Elemental Wisdom for Resolving Disputes and Transcending Differences* (Novato: New World Library, 2004), 99–100.

It's natural to be overwhelmed...Jerry White, *I Will Not Be Broken* (New York: St. Martin's Press, 2008), 53.

We can only be said to be alive...www.thinkexist.com.

In the twenty years after...Harold Kushner, *When Bad Things Happen to Good People* (New York: Anchor, 2004), xii.

Chapter 2: Get a Team

You cannot hope to build...Marie Curie, *Pierre Curie*, trans. Charlotte Kellogg and Vernon Lyman Kellogg (New York: Macmillan, 1923), 168.

Tough times can be considered...Malidoma Somé, *The Healing Wisdom of Africa* (New York: Tarcher, 1999), 279.

during the initiation rites into manhood...Although particular ritual tests may need to be accomplished alone, the community plays a pivotal role in initiations around the world. It sends off the initiate and, in some cultures, observes the rites. A priest, shaman, or elder guides the initiate through the process. Often there are fellow initiates. To complete the ritual, the initiate is incorporated back into the community by the community. For more information, see Arnold Van Gennep, *The Rites of Passage* (Chicago: University of Chicago Press, 1960), or Ronald L. Grimes, *Readings in Ritual Studies* (New York: Prentice Hall, 1995).

The state of Montana...John Grant Emeigh, "Suicide: Montana crying for help," *Montana Standard,* February 1, 2010, http://mtstandard.com/news/local/article_d8c9808b-5159-5717-a685-c443601192f5.html.

In the classic...Arnold Van Gennep, *The Rites of Passage* (Chicago: University of Chicago Press, 1960), xvii–xviii.

Longevity studies...Malcolm Gladwell, *Outliers: The Story of Success* (New York: Little, Brown and Company, 2008), 9–11. For more information on the Blue Zones longevity studies, go to www.bluezones.com.

The same expectation of support...African ritualist Malidoma Somé adds, "Dagara people don't comprehend the idea of private grief" (*The Healing Wisdom of Africa* [New York: Tarcher, 1999], 220). From the Jewish tradition, we learn the practice of sitting shiv'ah where friends provide constant company and support to the mourners for seven days. Even as a person dies, in many cultures, he or she is kept company through the last breath and is not left alone until days after. In Japan and among the Toraja of Sulawesi in Indonesia, for example, loved ones will bathe, watch over, and sleep near the corpse, speaking to their departed loved one as though they are still alive until internment (Hikaru Suzuki, "The Phase of Negated Death," in *Death, Mourning and Burial: A Cross-Cultural Reader*, ed. C. G. M. Robben [Oxford: Blackwell, 2004], 224, and Paul C. Rosenblatt, "Grief in small-scale societies," in *Death and Bereavement Across Cultures*, ed. Colin Murray Parkes [New York: Routledge, 2006], 28). In the Burmese Buddhist culture, the body is never left alone between death and cremation. While relatives cook, there "will also be a group of men gambling in the room where the body lies" (Kenneth Kramer, *The Sacred Art of Dying: How World Religions Understand Death* [New York: Paulist Press, 1988], 54).

What should young people...Kurt Vonnegut, "Thoughts of a Free Thinker," commencement address, Hobart and William Smith Colleges (May 26, 1974).

A man's growth is seen...Henry David Thoreau and Ralph Waldo Emerson, *The Complete Works of Ralph Waldo Emerson & Henry David Thoreau* (CreateSpace, 2008), 23.

I always felt that...Antony Alpers, *Katherine Mansfield: A Biography* (London: Jonathan Cape, 1954), 266.

The general support team role...Arnold Van Gennep, *The Rites of Passage* (Chicago: University of Chicago Press), 74–77, and Ronald L. Grimes, *Deeply into the Bone* (Berkeley: University of California Press, 2002), 138–41.

During her lifetime...Elizabeth Kübler-Ross, *Working It Through* (New York: Scribner, 1997), 56-57.

I am speaking now...Harriet Beecher Stowe, *Little Foxes* (1865), 121.

Trouble creates a capacity to handle it...Robert I. Fitzhenry, *The Harper Book of Quotations* (New York: Collins, 1993), 39.

Recovering from loss...Rosenblatt, "Grief in small-scale societies," 41.

Presence is a noun...Debbie Hall, "The Power of Presence," in *This I Believe*, 101.

Those who do not know...Golda Meir, interview with Oriana Fallaci, *Ms.*, April 1973.

Lots of people want to ride...www.brainyquote.com

Within traditional Tibetan...Uwe P. Gielen, "A death on the roof of the world: The perspective of Tibetan Buddhism," in *Death and Bereavement*, 80.

person's sense of humor...Gerald G. May, MD, *The Dark Night of the Soul* (San Francisco: Harper, 2005), 155-57.

Five (or more)...American Psychiatric Association, *Diagnostic and Statistical Manual of Mental Disorders, Fourth Edition, Text Revision: DSM-IV-TR* (Washington, D.C.: American Psychiatric Publishing, 2000a), 356.

Quoting author Judith Hooper...May, *Dark Night*, 158–59.

Chapter 3: Believe in a Happy Ending

The French philosopher...Robert Jay Lifton and Eric Olson, "Symbolic Immortality," in *Death, Mourning and Burial*, 34.

"little deaths,"...Kramer, *Sacred Art of Dying*, 188.

I am a more sensitive...Kushner, *When Bad Things Happen*, 179.

Positive psychologist...Baker, *What Happy People Know*, 93.

Let us weigh...Blaise Pascal, *Pensées*, trans. Roger Ariew (Indianapolis: Hackett Publishing, 2005), 212.

Many cultures strive...Kramer, *Sacred Art of Dying*, 76. Also in "A death on the roof of the world," *Death and Bereavement* author Uwe Gielen adds according to Shakyamuni Buddha, "Of all mindfulness meditations, that on death is supreme." Is life not like a bubble in a stream or a fleeting dream from which only the few awaken during meditation or, perhaps at the hour of their death?" (73–74). *The Tibetan Book of the Dead* or *Bardö T'ödröl* is "not only a book to help the dying; it is above all a guide for living." It teaches us "whatever is concrete, externally visible and therefore seemingly real is in truth only an illusion which sooner or later will fade away" (91).

Brain researchers...Mantras often invoke attitudes of learning, hope, and gratitude. Interestingly, all three of these responses must be processed in our neocortex, or the two hemispheres residing on the top of our heads. This is the portion of our brains best equipped for complex problem solving. When the neocortex is engaged, we have access to our creativity and can consider future implications of our actions. Meanwhile fear is handled by our brain stem, which doesn't want new information. To be able to adjust, to gather information about our situation, we want to appreciate our circumstances. Baker, *What Happy People Know*, 80, and Ratey, *A User's Guide*, 171–72.

All shall be well...Quoted in Maggie Oman Shannon, *Prayers for Healing: 365 Blessings, Poems, and Meditations from Around the World* (Berkeley: Conari Press, 2000), 150.

As Gandhi died...Kramer, *Sacred Art of Dying*, 27, 152.

Whether or not everything...The belief in the rightness of all things is ubiquitous. We find it in the concept of karma and interconnectedness in the Hindu and Buddhist traditions. It is found in the intimate involvement of angels and gods in our lives in Judaism and Christianity, and in the Greek and Roman traditions. David Bohm, the quantum physicist, calls this the implicate order of the universe. Bohm's theories state that in the universe there are no mistakes, and thus that everything happens for a reason. What appears chaotic, ridiculous, or wrong is in some way ordered, necessary, and right. Given our limited viewpoint, we may not necessarily be able to see the perfection (Michael Toms, "Wholeness, Creativity and Quantum Reality with David Bohm" from interview 1785 "Parts of a Whole," New Dimensions Media [Ukiah, 2006]).

"Everything happens for a reason"...Victor E. Frankl, *Man's Search for Meaning* (Boston: Beacon Press, 2006), 99.

In his seminal...Ibid., 155.

When prisoners...Ibid., 139.

On a particularly terrible day...Ibid., 73.

Meaning is a form...Rachel Naomi Remen, *My Grandfather's Blessings: Stories of Strength, Refuge and Belonging* (New York: Riverhead, 2000), 170.

Scientific research...Experiments show that we see only that for which we are searching. For more information, see K. C. Cole, *Mind Over Matter: Conversations with the Cosmos* (New York: Harcourt, 2003), 216–17, and K. C. Cole, *First You Build a Cloud and Other Reflections on Physics as a Way of Life* (New York: Harcourt Brace, 1999), 51.

Winter

When we fall...Kathleen McDonald, *How to Meditate* (Somerville: Wisdom Publications, 1984), 152.

In the sixteenth century...May, *Dark Night*, 33–36.

The Greeks gave...There is also a positive cross-cultural motif that arises from this darkness. In modern times, quantum physicists name the state where system is in chaos as "potentiality," or the state where new possibilities can arise. It is the soil from which all things can grow. For more information, see Fritjof Capra, *The Tao of Physics:*

An Exploration of the Parallels between Modern Physics and Eastern Mysticism (Boston: Shambhala, 1999), 222–23.

Philosophers and brain researchers...Plato, *The Allegory of the Cave* (CreateSpace, 2010).

The little reed...www.thinkexist.com.

In the African Dagara... Somé, *Healing Wisdom of Africa*, 220.

All things arise...Thomas Byrom, trans., *The Heart of Awareness: A Translation of the Ashtavakra Gita* (Boston: Shambhala, 1990), 28.

The advice for Winter...Combs, *Way of Conflict*, 128–29.

Chapter 4: Give Yourself a Break

And this is important...Howard Thurman, *Meditations of the Heart* (Boston: Beacon Press, 1981), 66.

Tough times are...Ratey, *A User's Guide*, 171–72.

The deeper that sorrow...Kahlil Gibran, *The Prophet* (Hertsfordshire: Wordsworth, 1996), 16.

The Jewish tradition...Kramer, *Sacred Art of Dying*, 135.

Among the Olo Ngaju...Hertz, *Death, Mourning and Burial*, 199, 200.

As difficult as it is...Elisabeth Kübler-Ross and David Kessler, *On Grief and Grieving: Finding the Meaning of Grief Through the Five Stages of Loss* (New York: Scribner, 2005), 24.

The Islamic, Hindu, Jewish...Jonathan Parry, "Sacrificial Death and the Necrophagous Ascetic," in *Death, Mourning and Burial*, 268, and http://www.chabad.org/library/article_cdo/aid/281541/jewish/The-Jewish-Way-in-Death-and-Mourning.htm

Around the world..."The many facets of Islam: Death, dying and disposal between orthodox rule and historical convention," in *Death and Bereavement*, 165.

When we love someone...Thomas Lewis, MD, Fari Amini, MD, and Richard Lannon, MD, *A General Theory of Love* (New York: Vintage, 2000), 94–96.

From the Islamic Sufi...Jelaluddin Rumi, *The Essential Rumi*, trans. Coleman Barks with John Moyne, A. J. Arberry, and Reynold Nicholson (San Francisco: HarperCollins, 1995), 109.

Don't cling to anything...Bhante Henepola Gunaratana, *Mindfulness in Plain English* (Somerville: Wisdom Publications, 2002), 40.

When his life falls...Stephen Mitchell, *The Book of Job* (New York: Harper, 1987), 95.

Shortly before...Kübler-Ross, *Grief and Grieving*, 12.

externalizes his anger...Kübler-Ross, *Working It Through*, 46.

uses communal water rituals...Somé, *Healing Wisdom of Africa*, 219–20.

Anthropologist Renato Rosaldo...Renato Rosaldo, "Grief and a Headhunter's Rage," in *Death, Mourning and Burial*, 167–71.

Rage is scary...Homer, *The Iliad*, trans. Robert Fagels (New York: Penguin, 1990), 495.

We are not permitted to choose... Dag Hammarskjold, *Markings*, trans. W. H. Auden and L. Fitzgerald Sioberg (New York: Vintage, 2006), 45.

In the Nyakyusa tribe...Rosaldo, *Death, Mourning and Burial*, 173, and Nigel Barley, *Grave Matters: A Lively History of Death around the World* (New York: Holt, 1995), 18.

My favorite anger-release...Phillip Moffit, *Dancing with Life: Buddhist Insights for Finding Meaning and Joy in the Face of Suffering* (New York: Rodale, 2008), 69.

How can you let...http://www.smashshack.com and http://money.cnn.com/2008/09/17/smallbusiness/smash_shack.smb/index.htm.

In the end...Donella Meadows, *Leverage Points: Places to Intervene in a System* (Hartland, Vt.: The Sustainability Institute, 1999), 19.

The goddess Inanna...Jean Shinoda Bolen, *Close to the Bone: Life Threatening Illness and the Search for Meaning* (New York: Scribner, 1996), 55–58.

As I walked to the square...Mitchell, *Book of Job*, 69.

In India...Parry, *Death, Mourning and Burial*, 273.

The practices of the Aghori...Ibid., 281.

To own one's own...Robert A. Johnson, *Owning Your Own Shadow: Understanding the Dark Side of the Psyche* (San Francisco: HarperCollins, 1991), 17.

As life becomes harder...Etty Hillesum, *An Interrupted Life* (New York: Holt, 1983), 166.

It is said that the demon...Tara Brach, *Radical Acceptance: Embracing your Life with the Heart of a Buddha* (New York: Bantam, 2003), 74–79.

Chapter 5: Eat, Drink, Play, Laugh

Imagination was given...www.thinkexist.com.

The wise see that...Eknath Easwaran, trans., *The Bhagavad Gita* (Berkeley: Nilgiri Press, 1985), 118.

When reviewing Richard Dowden's...http://www.oprah.com/book/Africa-Altered-States-Ordinary-Miracles-by-Richard-Dowdens

Africa lives...Richard Dowden, *Africa: Altered States, Ordinary Miracles* (New York: Public Affairs, 2009) 286–87.

All this hurrying...Rainer Maria Rilke, *In Praise of Mortality*, trans. and ed. Anita Barrows and Joanna Macy (New York: Riverhead Books, 2005), 99.

In Ancient Greece...Pittu Laungani, "Death in a Hindu Family," in *Death and Bereavement*, 57, and *Iliad*, 567–87.

When we play...Stuart Brown, MD, *Play: How It Shapes the Brain, Opens the Imagination, and Invigorates the Soul* (New York: Avery, 2009), 5.

probably the most important...Brown, *Play*, 6.

Brown defines play as follows...Ibid., 17–18.

Harvard researcher...Emily Hancock, *The Girl Within: A Groundbreaking New Approach to Female Identity* (New York: Fawcett Columbine, 1989), 8.

The personal life deeply lived...www.thinkexist.com.

Additionally, play...Brown, *Play*, 29–33, 44.

Indeed, thought which tries...David Bohm and F. David Peat, *Science, Order, and Creativity* (New York: Bantam, 1984), 45.

If I had no sense of humor...Combs, *Way of Conflict*, 146.

The Nyakyusa of Malawi...Barley, *Grave Matters*, 34–35 and Barbara Babcock, "Arrange Me into Disorder: Fragments and Reflections of Ritual Clowning," in *Readings in Ritual Studies* (New Jersey: Prentice Hall, 1996), 12.

One must have...Friedrich Nietzsche, *The Portable Nietzsche* (New York: Penguin, 1954), 129.

We joke with death...Barley, *Grave Matters*, 36.

Venerable Genyo...Gerry Shishin Wick, *The Book of Equanimity: Illuminating Classic Zen Koans* (Somerville: Wisdom Publications, 2005), 178.

Hopi and Zuni ritual clowns...Babcock, *Readings in Ritual Studies*, 8.

When a people can laugh...Vine Deloria Jr., *Custer Died for Your Sins* (New York: Macmillan, 1969), 168.

Another morning humor...For more information, go to www.laughteryoga.org.

Spring

In the depth of winter...Nathan A. Scott, *The Unquiet Vision: Mirrors of Man in Existentialism* (Cleveland: World Pub. Co., 1969), 116.

After the travels...Elizabeth Lesser, *Broken Open: How Difficult Times Can Help Us Grow* (New York: Villard, 2005), 49.

Cultural anthropologist...Angeles Arrien, *Second Half of Life* (San Francisco: Sounds True, 2006), 118–19.

To be nobody-but-yourself...E. E. Cummings, "A Poet's Advice to Students," in *A Miscellany*, ed. George James Firmage (New York: October House, 1965), 335.

Chapter 6: Celebrate

In the long haul...Grimes, *Deeply into the Bone*, 6.

why funerals and mourning rituals...Ibid., 218.

In 1929...Van Gennep, *Rites of Passage*, 11.

When discussing the Dagara...Sobonfu Somé, *The Spirit of Intimacy: Ancient Teachings in the Ways of Relationship* (Berkeley: Berkeley Hills, 1997), 28–32.

I celebrate myself... Walt Whitman, "Song of Myself," in *Walt Whitman's Song of Myself: A Sourcebook and Critical Edition* (New York: Routledge, 2005), 142.

Create a symbolic action... "The Tibetan Book of the Dead: A Way of Life and The Great Liberation (Alive Mind, 1994), DVD.

I believe in always going... Deirdre Sullivan, "Always go to the funeral," in *This I Believe*, 235–37.

It "attunes" us... Grimes, *Deeply into the Bone*, 13.

Chapter 7: Mark the End and a New Beginning

Art will remain... Jane Waller, *The Human Form in Clay* (Ramsbury: Crowood Press, 2001), 98.

the three phases... Van Gennep, *Rites of Passage*, 11.

new names are also given... Grimes, *Deeply into the Bone*, 106.

How do you explain... Thomas Moore, *Dark Nights of the Soul: A Guide to Finding Your Way through Life's Ordeals* (New York: Gotham, 2004), 9–10.

John of the Cross used... May, *Dark Night*, 147, 182.

The authors of the book of Job...Mitchell, *Book of Job*, 21, 88.

International consultant and artist...For more information and tips from Mary Corrigan, go to http://www.creativity4us.com.

"I believe in a broad definition...Frank X Walker, "Creative Solutions to Life's Challenges," in *This I Believe*, 251.

The imagination is a great...John O'Donohue, *Anam Cara* (New York: HarperCollins, 1997), 145.

"it is impossible to separate...Patricia Janis Broder, *Hopi Painting: The World of the Hopis* (New York: E. P. Dutton, 1978), 7.

"Where there is creating...Juan Mascaro, trans., *The Upanishads* (New York: Penguin, 1965), 119.

Art is, at last...Daniel Ladinsky, trans., *The Gift—Poems by Hafiz, The Great Sufi Master* (New York: Penguin, 1999), 52.

Educator and author...Matthew Fox, *Creation Spirituality: Liberating Gifts for the Peoples of the Earth* (San Francisco: HarperCollins, 1991) 98–99.

I believe that what we often...Frank X Walker, "Creative Solutions to Life's Challenges, in *This I Believe*, 250.

*"Sometimes a wound...*Remen, *Grandfather's Blessings*, 25–26.

*"If you spend some time thinking ...*His Holiness the Dalai Lama and Howard C. Cutler, *The Art of Happiness: A Handbook for Living* (New York: Penguin, 1998), 137.

*Changing the hair...*Effie Bendann, *Death Customs: An Analytical Study of Burial Rites* (White Fish, Montana: Kessingler, 2010), 89–92.

Summer

*An optimist isn't necessarily...*Martin Keogh, ed., *Hope Beneath Our Feet: Restoring Our Place in the Natural World* (Berkeley: North Atlantic Books, 2010), 279.

*This is a global...*In the Greek myth of Demeter, after the goddess Persephone spent time with Hades under the earth, she too was required to sacrifice and spend winters as the Queen of the Underworld. There are also the common practices of sending money, figurines, and even other living beings along with a corpse to pay for passage through the depths. It seems we are expected to furnish something to be able to make it to our next life.

Chapter 8: Give Back to Come Back

A survey of 6,360...Dr. Andrew Weil, *Self Healing Newsletter*, July 2009, 1.

Many persons have a wrong idea...Helen Keller, "The Simplest Way to Be Happy," *Home Magazine*, February 1933.

Sharing or sacrifice...In some cultures, widows or parents who have lost children are given prescribed jobs to support the passage of the soul of a loved one through its transitory period. Also, intricate ceremonies and daily rituals globally ensure that the spirit finds its next home or resting place. In Greece, grieving women are expected to visit the cemetery once or twice a day and clean the gravesites of their husbands, parents, or children. Together the women light candles, pray, and lament their loss. Grieving is actively performed daily for five years until the bones are exhumed. The loved ones then count each bone and a priest pours red wine over the skeleton, which is placed in a box in an ossuary. After this closing celebration, a remembrance is held on Soul Saturdays and other holidays for those who have died. The dead are believed to need company, light, and homes; hence the visiting of the cemetery, the candles, and the care of the gravesite. Grimes, *Deeply into the Bone*, 249.

The nectar of life...Maximillian Hodder, "A New Birth of Freedom," in *This I Believe,* 125.

In the Pacific Northwest...Sergei Kan, "The Nineteenth-Century Tlingit Potlatch: A New Perspectives," in *Death, Mourning and Burial,* 288.

"While I lay in...*Alcoholics Anonymous: The Big Book*, 4th ed. (Center City, Minn.: Hazelden, 2002), 14.

Jerry White, who...White, *I Will Not Be Broken*, 2.

One of the deep secrets of life...www.goodreads.com.

Tibetan Buddhists...Gielen, *Death and Bereavement*, 82, and Kramer, *Sacred Art of Dying*, 72–77.

As I look more deeply...Thich Nhat Hahn, *Heart of Understanding* (Berkeley: Parallax, 2009), 19.

In 1927, Buckminster Fuller...Phil Patton, "A 3-Wheel Dream That Died at Takeoff," *New York Times*, June 15, 2008, and http://www.nytimes.com/2008/06/15/automobiles/collectibles/15BUCKY.html.

I was lucky enough...Deidre Combs, *Worst Enemy, Best Teacher: How to Survive and Thrive with Opponents, Competitors and the People Who Drive You Crazy* (Novato: New World Library, 2005), 160.

*Many spiritual traditions call...*Kramer, *Sacred Art of Dying*, 23, 35.

*Financial guru Warren Buffett...*Bill Gates, "Unleashing the Power of Creativity," in *This I Believe*, 72, and Brown, *Play*, 63.

*Some offer wealth...*Easwaran, *Bhagavad Gita*, 120.

*Mirabai Bush advises...*Gail Straub, *Rhythm of Compassion* (Boston: Journey Editions, 2000), 90–91.

*Mirroring Bush's advice...*Remen, *My Grandfather's Blessings*, 12.

*Look for what has heart...*Angeles Arrien, *The Four-Fold Way: Walking the Paths of the Warrior, Teacher, Healer, and Visionary* (San Francisco: HarperSanFrancisco, 1993), 8.

*"Give, give, give...*Isabel Allende, "In Giving I Connect with Others," in *This I Believe*, 14–15.

*"Our basic convictions...*Margaret Singer, "When Children Are Wanted," in *This I Believe*, 210.

*A young Alaskan woman...*Mary Cook, "The Hardest Work You'll Ever Do,"in *This I Believe*, 37–38.

We confuse attachment with love...Kathleen McDonald, *How to Meditate* (Somerville: Wisdom Publications, 1984), 99.

The martial artists call...Moore, *Dark Nights*, 196.

Tough-Times Classics

Success is not measured by what you accomplish...www.thinkexist.com

I would suggest...Mitchell, *Book of Job*.

ACKNOWLEDGMENTS

Of the books I have written, this one took the most time and was the toughest to complete. Note: watch what you name things!

As with venturing through tough times, a compiled team helped ease a rocky journey. I want to thank Amanda Larrinaga, Kevin Connolly, Bruce Combs, Deborah McAtee, F. Craig Barber and Maribeth Goodman, who served as guides, reading every word and offering insightful comments. I deeply appreciate the brave friends and clients who inspired this book and shared their personal tough-times stories. Maribeth and Tony Goodman were also great fellow travelers as they passed along new publishing options and opportunities. A vast and compassionate caring community cheered for my progress. I am especially grateful for Angeles Arrien, Carmen McSpadden, Karly Randolph Pitman, Diana and Marcus Stevens, and Justine Willis Toms, who provided perfect encouragement just when I needed it.

ABOUT THE AUTHOR

Deidre Combs is the author of *The Way of Conflict: Elemental Wisdom for Resolving Disputes and Transcending Differences* and *Worst Enemy, Best Teacher: How to Survive and Thrive with Opponents and the People Who Drive You Crazy*. She provides personal development and cross-cultural conflict skills as a consultant, coach, mediator, and professor. Combs has worked with a variety of corporate, government, NGO, and individual clients, including the U.S. Forest Service, U.S. Postal Service, IBM, and Aveda Corporation.

Since 2007, she has taught intensive leadership training to Montana State University students and State Department-selected student and professional leaders from throughout the Middle East, Africa, Asia, Eastern Europe, Latin America, and Pakistan's FATA region.

Combs holds a doctorate focused on world religions from UCS/Naropa University and lives in the Rocky Mountain West.

Made in the USA
Charleston, SC
27 June 2013